The Yearbook Book

BY **IAN SUMMERS**

WITH A FOREWORD BY
JACK PONTIFELL

BALLANTINE BOOKS / NEW YORK, NEW YORK

1

Library of Congress Catalog Card Number: 75-44321
ISBN 0-345-24732-9-595

Manufactured in the United States of America
First Edition: April, 1976

Boosters

Alan Shapiro   Diane Strong   Dianne Smith   Richard Carino

Jean Simason   Nancy Lufan   Mike Summers   James Petracca   Allan Lopata

Jean Barnard   Dorothy O'Neill   Charley Hochkyppel   Carol Paret

Beverly Rhodes   Patricia Hardy   Barbara De Ritter   James Storoysk   Kenneth Pere

Marilyn Wola   Helen Steele   Marge Kelley   Carol Van Dyk   Marilyn Mickens

Bob

— Dedication —

for Rochelle, Amy, Shaun, my parents who started it all, and the entire Fair Lawn High Class of '57

Stuart Wasserlauf   Pat Freeling   Ray Becker   Linda Kamerling   Valerie Van Blaik

Sam Berman   Lois Fox   Richard (Gung Ho) Pat   Grayce Rosso   Alan Mingrae

Bruce B Shaw   Sondra De Petro   Carol Conte   Beverly Nightman   Barbara Miller

Howie Phillips   Philip Bralow   Tomey Christoph   Jack Sisco   Ina Nachinson

Mary Porelle   Lois Bugatto   Pat Sheppard   Rose Paciello   Lois Lombardi

Bill Coe   Judith Schneider   Marvin Weisburg   Anita Solinsky   "DICK" HERTZ

Alice Garella   Ken Bacon   Mary Lou Croft   Joan Lacher

Adrian   Patti Walsh   Ralph Pine   Adrienne Camp   Hedwig Kotz

Elizabeth Kutzo   Steve Schein   Arlene Ransom   Stanley Stein   John Sisco

JOAN LEVINE   Art Lowenstein   Harvey Sapolow   Bob Donato   Fred Becker

Joanne Tiol   Sandy Dudas   Barry Froelih   Jean Schmidt   Bill Smith

Jackie Hand   Joan Schulman   Bob Piccola   George 'Ibis' Naugle   Jackie Winns

Ed Allen

GWEN BERDY   Barbara King Freistman   (NAVY)   Jean Sensen   Alice Toloma

Susan Frard   Alan Gottlieb   George Buchner   Paul Strosch / Bob Claeksen   Ann Spinella

Sally Ginsberg   Jerry Wiltern   Dick Heiss   Irwin Schwartz   Connie Zurich

Judy Solomon   Alfred Klein   Sandy Holando   Larry Freemauer   Dixie Jaynes

Philip Teitel   Gary Schadewald   Betty Schaefer   Marie Laure   Jane Seamon

Carole Morion   Pat Surmonte   Alan De Old   Barbara Guozzo   Diana

Nancy Lade   Alan F. Newman   Albert Miller   Guennie Marcalus   R.K.B.

FOREWORD

When Ian Summers first asked me to write the introduction to this absurd book, I concluded once again that he was mad.

A yearbook book indeed! How cute. How banal. How littered with lust for a buck. Who needed it? Who wanted it? To me a yearbook book was merely another non-book book.

But you don't understand, said Ian.

That is the point, he said. And he was right. For as I
turned the pages of yearbook after yearbook, I
came to realize that the power of my words was
defeating, and that in those anonymous faces there
was truth.
Painfully I opened the pages of my own yearbook
and looked into that unrecognizable face that my
name told me had once been mine.

Who would want to open pages from the past and
look back at mirror images that remind one of lost
innocence and youth undone? Who would want to
be reminded of dreams gone awry? To gaze upon
those yearbook faces, those subway station photo-
graphs of massed youth, those postage stamp
hopes—to gaze upon them and to compare them to
the grim realities of the decades following? Yuck. It is
enough to give me the foxtrots, I said.
And even worse, I said, if a person were to like
himself or herself today—how could he or she bear
to look back into those acned eyes of the teens,
either terrified by things to come, or deceived—by
ragtime or jitterbugging or goldfish eating or back-
seat fucking or demonstrating—into thinking they
were going to enter a better world?
Those who have aged well don't want to look back.
And those who have lost it don't want to be
reminded, Ian. Don't you see?

I understand only too well,' I replied. A yearbook
book is more grist for those dreary devourers of
trivia—those poor, starved outsiders who want
inside. Those collectors of non-information who gain
personality and front for their non-beings by
digesting potsful of gossip and who spew it back to
gain power and presence for their non-being selves.
This is a book for assassins, I said. For Oswalds and
Sirhans and Bremers. For all those Mansonites who
play horse chestnuts with life, who amass power
through the possession of nada. Look at me, they say,
I'm powerful. I know Rock Hudson was really named
Roy Fitzgerald and that James Stewart once drew
pictures and played the accordion.
After all, I asked, why do all of those high school and
college yearbooks sit gathering dust on shelves with
pages unopened and memories buried?

Not long ago, I visited the teacher of my seven-year-
old son for a report on his progress in school. In the
course of our meeting she demonstrated a technique
she had used to create an awareness of growth
through accomplishment. She had collected a
sampling of drawings he had done, and at a certain
moment toward the end of the school year she
showed them to him. The early ones first, and then
the later ones. He looked at the drawings with a
feeling of strangeness—regarding them as the work
of an impostor. The later drawings filled him with
pride. Looking at them side by side he was able to
recognize growth in himself, in the way he had
drawn himself not as a stick but as a person next to a
tree, how in the later drawings he had taken
possession of that world which he had created. She
did the same with letters of the alphabet and
numbers. He sensed that in that one year he had
expanded and grown and earned the right to be
seven instead of six.

That is the way yearbooks work.

Could our teachers have conned us into this ritual
only for nothing? No, they knew.

The reason for a yearbook's being is as a kind of
ballast against the erosion of time. Why else all that
lining up for photos, all that detail, all that rhetoric?
Certainly the windy valedictories cannot be the
justification. Nor the forgotten graffiti. Our teachers
must have known that that sentimental syrup really
meant something after all. You see, if education has
any message—and I think it does—then there has to
be reason for the ritual being carried on for so long.
Really study yearbooks, and you see that they
haven't changed very much from the turn of the
century till now. The dead war heroes look out at you
accusingly no matter which war it was. The cheers
are the same. The principal's message is as one. If
you've seen one yearbook, you've seen them all.
Except your own.

BOBBY (OH ROCKET) SHORT

Your own yearbook contains faces you dimly
remember. Teachers you hated and teachers you
crushed on. Plays you saw. Loves you lost. Games
you played.

But what of this yearbook book? Ian, you're not
conning us either. Are you?

Looking into someone else's yearbook is like going
to a funeral. Secretly you're glad it isn't yours.

But look a little deeper. Look into the face of the
youthful Gregory Peck. It hasn't changed much, has
it? He was who he is. Even then you would have
wanted him on your side. Look at little Theodosia
Goodman out there in California God-knows-where.
Read what they said about her. Could you have
known who she'd be?

Oh, there is a challenge in this book after all.

Look at Bobby Short. Was the difference written over
him even then? I think it was.

Look at Allen Ginsberg. What mother wouldn't have
wanted her daughter to bring him home?
Now I understand why one of the most famous of
our nation's news commentators said no to this book.
His face revealed nothing of who he'd become. How
painful for him to look back into that abyss. At sixty
his mirror is more gratifying.
Flip the pages of the *Yearbook Book* fast. See the
cheerleaders jump. And rah-rah. And root.
Ian, you've done it. I think you've done it.
Is that the face of Walter Matthau? Even then a
cement mixer was working on it. Hold a match up to
it and maybe you'll see Vesuvius erupt.

You have been a good office boy But you never could remember to bring those excuses. Best of Luck.

Perhaps there should have been more about the teachers. They weren't really so bad.

To freeze for eternity that Latin teacher who wept when she heard the class outcast suddenly translate Cicero superbly. Or the legendary teacher at Washington Irving High School who back in the nineteen teens would sit before her class with a giant pot of Vaseline always at her fingertips. Regularly she'd finger a glob and eat it. And no one ever knew why. She probably liked it. Or the teacher of Dramatic English who would save her finest words of praise for utterance only twice a year. "A sheer delight," she'd say and someone would swell with pride forever.

And the coach. There was always the coach, and somehow he'd always try to be Knute Rockne, but to us he was always Pat O'Brien.

But they exist only in memory.

Someday, maybe there will even be a musical
Yearbook Book.
A young poet named Edward Planer, fresh out of
school and on his way to the Korean War, wrote an
article for the Saturday Review called "Hail to Thee
Our Alma Miller."
As he grew up, Glenn Miller was the man, and
Eddie's point was that, for him, high school memories
would always be replayed to the background music
of his times.
Ah, for that young poet it was the sweet sound of
"Moonlight Serenade" created for dancing close—
back then when people touched.
My God, what other sounds there have been!
"K-K-K-Katie." And "Cement Mixer." And "Jeepers
Creepers."

Dear Miss Thomas,
You're one of the
best English Teachers
I have ever had.
You made it all
very interesting
Thank you,

Look into the faces of the Yearbook Book and hear
them sing "Flat Foot Floozie with a Floy Floy." Or are
they listening to that genius Fats, singing "Your Socks
Don't Match"?
I remember how Isaac Rosenfeld, a superb and
too-soon-dead writer, took a group of kids fresh out
of high school to a small-town nightclub and
announced, "Tonight we are all going to dig Diz."
And we dug. We Bee-Bopped and we Bop-Beeped
till dawn.
Listen to it, darling, that was our song…
There were some of us, a handful maybe, back in the
thirties and forties, who dug folk songs and songs
of protest and blues. Woody Guthrie. Leadbelly.
Richard Dyer-Bennet. Josh White.

The Washable Blues
Words by Ron Rosenberg—Music by Arlo Guthrie

I've been working on this paper now for so many days
This washable blue is takin' permanent ways
To know me when you see me you would not have to think
I've got long boney fingers and they're covered with ink.

Chorus:
I've got the washable blues
I've got the washable blues
You'll turn yellow from smoking
or brown from booze,
But nothing's goin' to stain you like the washable blues.

If I die in college, when my soul begins to sink
There'll be nothing to blame but the paper and ink
And while I lie a dying in the damp of morning's dew
The rot on my belly will be washable blue.

And so I'm here to warn you all and listen to my song
I ain't so good at writing so a lot of things are wrong
But there's one thing I can tell you, about what not and what to do.
Don't waste your time a writing about washable blue.

But the music changed. Because soon kids had to
ask themselves new questions when they got out of
school.

Should they chance Vietnam or should they go to
Canada? Was this land really our land from California to the New York island? Or was it all bought
up?

There were still nonsense songs. But they meant that
nothing made sense. There were still protest songs,
but they didn't just get sung in a living room to the
scent of Mom's pie. They went with tear gas. And real
tears.

The lines were funny but they were searing. The
Beatles knew that nothing matched.

God, they were angry and brittle and bright! In my
time there was a poet named Dylan who made
beautiful sounds. Later, there was another poet
named Dylan who turned kids inside out.

And while Woody wrote songs about how we all
had to fight back, his little son Arlo wrote about how
he kept from fighting anyone.

Now everyone's touching again. I guess we need it.
But for every generation there are things we'd prefer
not to remember. When someone asked Virgil
Thomson, the great composer and music critic, for his
yearbook, he delivered it obligingly. But his picture
wasn't in it. The school regretted that he had been at
war.

We didn't even try to get the picture of a big,
redheaded Massachusetts kid named Butch. He was
from the to-be-or-not-to-be generation. If he went to
Canada, he'd be doing what he believed to be right.
But in his little town, his parents would be disgraced.
So he went to Vietnam. And cheerfully he told
people how he chose helicopter service because
lots of people would be commuting to the beautiful
Berkshires and they would need him.

13

BARBARA MARIE PAYNE
Fairfax High.

RAY WILLIAM PETERS
Roosevelt. Football. University of Washington. Train Engineer.

ELDRED GREGORY PECK
St. Johns Military Academy. Adv. Glee, Boys' Hi Jinx, Class B Football, Interclass Football, Interclass Baseball. State.

ROBERT E. PETERSON

ELBERT PHILIP PEDERSON
Roosevelt. Adv. Band, Gens de Guerre. 1st Sergeant and Lieutenant R.O.T.C., Usher Mgr. Draftsman.

THEODORE J. PFATENHAUER
Roosevelt. State. Accountant.

RUTH PAULINE PEMBERTON
Roosevelt. Girl Reserves, G.A.A., Secretary of G.A.A., Student Coach.

JEANETTE PHILBRICK

FRANK PENUELAS
Memorial. Class B Football, Varsity Football, Varsity S. Wrestling, Class B Basketball. U.C.L.A. Coach.

DOROTHY HOPE POLLARD
Bennett High, New York. University of Buffalo. Laboratory Technician.

ROSE MARIE PEREZ
Roosevelt. Library. State.

MORRIS POLLOCK
Memorial. Football, Track, Vice-President Sr. A. Class. State. Coaching.

JUNE, 1933

It seemed as if he'd hardly left when news came back
that he'd been blown up. In a chopper. What a bum
rap. No one took the rap for him the way they did for
the President who sent him there.

So don't look for Virgil Thomson's picture in the
Yearbook Book. And don't look for Butch. Mr.
Thomson sent his regrets, but no one had the
courage to ask Butch's mother to open his yearbook
once more and express hers.

There are a lot of wars in this book. Do you think you
can find them?

And so the famed faces do have meaning, Ian. They
do, of course, compel us because of our contem-
porary fascination with winners, and though they
turn us into paparazzi, they also permit us to rate
ourselves, to see how we've stacked up in time's dirty
game.
But there is also a gnawing hole in the gut that
reminds us of the others, those fameless faces that
stare out at us from these pages. What ever became
of them?
Well, let's hope that someone out there remembers.
I think we're going to enjoy the *Yearbook Book.*
So thank you, Ian.
The only thing left when we have absorbed it all and
had our fun is for each of us to approach the dusty
bookshelf and to take down the yearbook
that surely sits there.

Take down your yearbook. And open it.
If you dare.

Principal's Message

THE daily activities of busy boys and girls on a high school campus are indicative of the spirit of a school. Every school is a city in miniature. It contains all the elements of a larger unit of organization. It offers opportunities for education in human relationships that train for adult living and participation in a democracy. The progressive school will make use of campus activities as a laboratory for teaching the art of living together harmoniously, constructively, and joyfully.

It is one of the chief aims and objectives of Van Nuys High School to provide varied and wholesome activities whereby students may engage in co-operative experiences of planning, working, and playing together—experiences in which helpful friendships may be formed as well as habits of altruism, loyalty, and courage—activities in which democratic practices may be fostered and the great objective of thinking with and for others and at the same time thinking for oneself inculcated.

DONNA H. HUBBARD.

Faculty Quotations

MME. FORTIER..............Are you in the sixth grade or are you in the sixth year?

MME. ROTTACH..............Je vous parlerai du 17ième siècle

MME. ROBERT..............You will fail and I will laugh. Ha! Ha!

MISS TAGGART..............This is a scream. C-

MISS WOOD..............X° does equal 1

MISS BLAIR..............I shouldn't want any girl of mine to get 100 on a College Board!

MISS LAWRENCE..............Is Susan absent again?

MISS RAYNOR..............(on the 26th of September) Take a good look at this, for you may not see it again before College Boards.

MISS GULICK..............I wish to see the following girls at noon today

MISS JONES..............It was not I who sent for you, it was Miss Gulick

MISS FLAGG..............Whisper it

MR. O'STEEN..............What a beautiful progression!

MR. LOCKHART..............Are you telling me or are you asking me?

MISS ALDRICH..............Now where would you look that up?

MISS HARDEN..............I don't mean to interrupt, but—

MISS CRANDON..............Thurfore it is thus 'n so!

FACULTY..............We hate to bring it up, but how many girls here are planning to take College Boards?

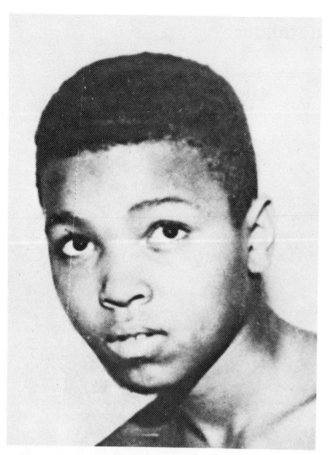

MUHAMMAD ALI

Cassius Marcellus Clay III
Central High School
Louisville, Kentucky

STEVE ALLEN

Steve Allèn
Mt. Carmel High School
Chicago, Illinois

enthusiastic

DUANE ALLMAN

Duane Allman
Class of 1965
Seabreeze Senior High School
Daytona Beach, Florida

GREGG ALLMAN

Gregg Allman
Class of 1965
Seabreeze Senior High School
Daytona Beach, Florida

ISAAC ASIMOV

Isaac Asimov
Class of 1935
Boys High School
New York, New York

Columbia, Surgeon. Grade Advisers Assistant
'33; Repair Squad; Typist for Biologist '35;
Honor Roll 5 times; Psychology Club.

*"When he looked at the clock, not only did it
stop, but it started going backwards."*

CHET ATKINS

Chester Atkins
Mountain Hill School
Hamilton, Georgia

FRANKIE AVALON

Frankie Avalone
South Philadelphia High School
Philadelphia, Pennsylvania

Mr. Summers
Best wishes go to a
great teacher...
Zounds of luck,
love & happiness.
May you
always have
the best...

21

THEDA BARA

Theodosia D. Goodman
Class of 1905
Walnut Hills High School
Cincinnati, Ohio

Dramatic Club; Gleam Staff. Theo excels in the literary art, and her work bears the stamp of true genius. Her literary ability, however, is not the only claim she has to those who have witnessed a performance of the Senior Dramatic Club. She is an entertaining conversationalist.

"With heart and fancy all on fire,
To climb the hill of fame."

ELVIN BISHOP

Elvin Richard Bishop
Class of 1960
Will Rogers High School
Tulsa, Oklahoma

⊘NLY — ♡YEST'DAY:—

"BERTIE" CAVIOR

THE YOUNG CHAIR-LADIES BESSIE CLEIF → AND GAYNELL ← ZIGARELLI

MURIEL AND HOSSEY

"LILLY" DE PASQUALE

"ETKALLEH" FISHER LUNCH HOUR...

MINNIE AND DOLLY—

JACKIE AND HIS MAMMA

"LITTLE MOE" GORDON

NITA — KITA

GOLDIE "LOOKS" CORN

HELENA VANDER ELS, WATCHIN' THE BIRDY

THE PUCH TWINS

"MOTEL" KANDELL, PLAYING WITH "TEDDY"

BILL BLASS

William Blass
Class of 1940
South Side High School
Fort Wayne, Indiana

Art; Booster; Times; Totem; Decoration
chairman for sophomore and junior banquets.

"Bill."

MEL BROOKS

Melvin Kaminsky
Class of 1944
Eastern District High School
Brooklyn, New York

Leadership is displayed by speech and thought!

CAROL BURNETT

Carole Burnett
Class of Winter 1951
Hollywood High School
Hollywood, California

VIKKI CARR

Florence Cardona
Rosemead High School
Rosemead, California

JOHNNY CARSON

John Carson
Class of 1943
Norfolk Senior High School
Norfolk, Nebraska

Minute Men 1, 2, 3, 4; Thespians 4;
Allied Youth 4; Hi-Y 1, 2, 3, 4;
features Milestone 4; features Political 4;
Orpheum 1, 2, 4.

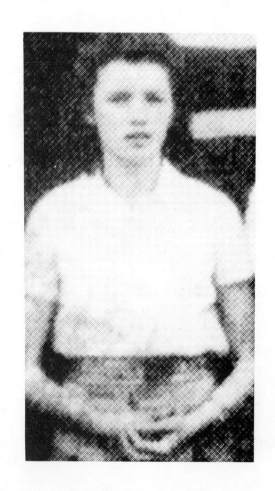

JUNE CARTER

June Carter
Hilton High School
Hilton, Virginia

CHUBBY CHECKER

Ernest Evans
Class of 1960
South Philadelphia High School
Philadelphia, Pennsylvania

Ernie, known to his record fans as "Chubby Checkers," is like so many other South Philadelphia entertainers who have gone a long way in a short time. He made teenagers rock with his record of "The Class." Ernie is at his best when he imitates "Fats Domino."

TONY CURTIS

Bernard Schwartz
Seward Park High School
New York, New York

"A good dancer, a good soldier and a good sport."

MAC DAVIS

Mac Davis
Class of 1958
Tom S. Lubbock High School
Lubbock, Texas

Hi-Y '58; TNT (science) '57;
Home Room President '56-'58.

Good times are enjoyed by all!

DAWN

Joyce Elaine Vincent
Class of 1965
John J. Pershing High School
Detroit, Michigan

NEIL DIAMOND

Neil Diamond
Class of 1956
Lincoln High School
Brooklyn, New York

Fencing team; G.O. councilman;
Choral; Sing; Class nite.

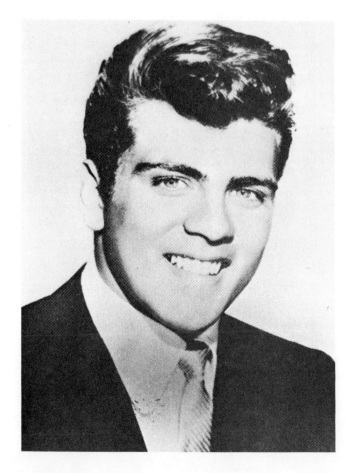

FABIAN

Fabian Forte
Class of 1961
South Philadelphia High School
Philadelphia, Pennsylvania

Fabian's favorite pastimes are horseback riding, swimming and
playing football with his two younger brothers and friends in the
neighborhood. He also enjoys traveling and is looking forward to
visiting Europe and the Far East as both an entertainer and tourist.
As for the future, he hopes to continue his career as an actor and
singer and further his education taking special college courses in
liberal arts and business administration.

LAWRENCE FERLINGHETTI

L. Furling Monsanto
Class of 1937
Mount Hermon School
Mount Hermon, Massachusetts

Basketball '35, '36, '37; Outdoor Track '35, '36;
Cross-Country '35; Junior League '34; Lyceum;
Players: HERMONITE Board.

"Moose"

Enthusiasm is needed in science and math!

EDDIE FISHER

Eddie Fisher
South Philadelphia High School
Philadelphia, Pennsylvania

GERALD FORD

Gerald Ford
Central High School
Grand Rapids, Michigan

National Honor Society; Student Council;
Inter-Hi Council; Sodalitas Latina; Glee Club;
Varsity Club; Football, Captain; Football,
Second Team; Basketball, First Team; Track;
Photo Committee.

GEORGE FOREMAN

George Foreman
E.O. Smith High School
Marshall, Texas

MAX FRANKEL

Max Frankel
Class of 1948
High School of Music and Art
New York, New York

ALTHEA GIBSON

Althea Gibson
Williston Industrial High School
Wilmington, North Carolina

ALLEN GINSBERG

Allen Ginsberg
Class of 1943
Eastside High School
Paterson, New Jersey

"Professor" is the philosopher and genius of the class...hopes to study law...Talent Club President; Criterion; Big Brother; Senior Mirror...fiend for Beethoven and Charlie Chaplin...indulges in music, politics, history, literature...Gold "P"...hates dull teachers and Republicans.

But seriously, my lambie pie — I think you're simply grand.

To Allen: — This odd little fellow worked on the Senior Mirror and seemed to think 'twas his job to make a gal think cleaner. He heckled and he ribbed me Til no more comes ? Stena —

ISRAEL GOLDSTEIN

Israel Goldstein
Class of 1911
Southern High and Manual Training
High School
Philadelphia, Pennsylvania

Born, June 18, 1896
Former school, Mt. Vernon.
Activities: Class Secretary ('11);
Class Orator.

"I:" "Ego:" "Myself"

Good grades are a must!

ARLO GUTHRIE

Arlo Guthrie
Class of 1965
The Stockbridge School
Interlaken, Massachusetts

BUDDY HACKETT

Leonard Hacker
New Utrecht High School
Brooklyn, New York

"There's laughs whenever he's around."

JIM HAGER

Jim Hager
Class of 1959
Maine Township High School East
Park Ridge, Illinois

Rifle Club 2; Variety Show 3.

JOHN HAGER

John Hager
Class of 1959
Maine Township High School East
Park Ridge, Illinois

Parking Lot Monitor 4; Intramurals 2, 3, 4;
Senior Acc. 3; Class Council Rep. 4;
Rifle Club 3.

MONTE HALL

Monte Halparin
Class of 1936
St. John's High School
Winnipeg, Manitoba

JOHN HAMMOND

John Paul Hammond
Class of 1960
The Marvelwood School
Cornwall, Connecticut

Entered Marvelwood September 1957.
Soccer '57, '58, '59; Basketball '58, '59, '60;
Lacrosse '58, '59, '60; Tennis '58, '59, '60;
Blue and White '57-'60; School Store '58-'60;
Yearbook '59-'60; Dramatics '59, '60;
Dance Committee '57-'58, '58-'59;
Blue Notes '57-'60; Dorm Supervisor '59-'60.

TOMMY HARPER

Tommy Harper
Class of 1958
Encinal High School
Alameda, California

Varsity Baseball; Varsity Basketball;
Varsity Football; Student Council; J.V.
Football; Adv. Office.

"This guy is really on the beam.
He's wanted on any team."

JOHN HARTFORD

John Cowan Harford
Class of 1956
John Burroughs School
Clayton, Missouri

Tenth grade: Rifle Club, Painting, Shop, "B"
Football, "B" Soccer, "B" Baseball. Eleventh
grade: Shop, "B" Football, "A" Soccer, "B"
Baseball. Twelfth grade: Painting Shop,
Mechanical Drawing, "A" Soccer, "A" Baseball.

Harf, who has been with us since seventh grade, is known far and
wide for his skill on the five-string banjo. His banjo playing and
singing with the Missouri Ridgerunners have been a welcome
addition to many Burroughs functions, parties, and outside affairs,
such as the National Folk Festival. His musical talents do not stop
with the banjo, for he can also pick the tar out of the guitar, fiddle,
and mandolin. B.H. is an excellent artist and an expert on
Mississippi River steamboats: if he is not making music with the
Ridgerunners he can often be found talking with some of his
steamboating friends downtown. B.H. has contributed much to
Burroughs, and we know he will be a success at college.

DOUG HENNING

Doug Henning
Class of 1966
Oakville Trafalgar High School
Oakville, Ontario

"I'm gonna lay off and haul ya one!"

CHARLTON HESTON

Charlton Heston
Class of 1941
New Trier High School
Winnetka, Illinois

Wilmette; Honor Groups 2, 3; Football 1, 2;
"Whappin' Wharf" 1; "Trelawney of the
Wells" 3; "Death Takes a Holiday" 4;
"The American Way" 4; Inklings Staff 3;
Art League 1, 2, 3, Vice-President 3;
Drama Club 1, 2, 3, 4; Broadcasting Club 3, 4;
Rifle Club 1, 2.

"Chuck"

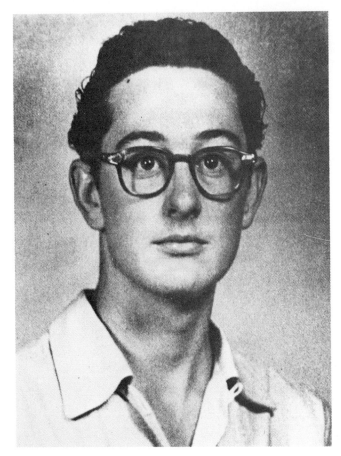

BUDDY HOLLY

Buddy Holly
Lubbock High School
Lubbock, Texas

ELIZABETH HOLTZMAN

Elizabeth Holtzman
Lincoln High School
Brooklyn, New York

Vice-President of G.O.; Girl leader of Jr.
Arista; Secretary of Arkon; Log; Forum;
Vice-President of National Honor Society.

Seniors save

BOB HOPE

Leslie Townes Hope
East High School
Cleveland, Ohio

ROCK HUDSON

Roy Fitzgerald
Class of 1943
New Trier High School
Winnetka, Illinois

Winnetka: Swimming 1, 2;
IM Baseball 1, 2; Volleyball 1, 2, 3;
Glee Club 1, 2; Geography 1, 2;
Manual Arts, Los Angeles, California 3.

for college!

JIM "CATFISH" HUNTER

James August Hunter
Class of 1964
Perquimans High School
Perquimans, North Carolina

Baseball 1, 2, 3, 4; Football 1, 2, 3, 4;
Monogram Club 2, 3, President 4;
Bus Drivers Club 3, 4; BEST LOOKING.

"Jimmy"

STACY KEACH

Stacy Keach
Class of 1959
Van Nuys High School
Van Nuys, California

SALLY KELLERMAN

Sally Kellerman
Class of 1955
Hollywood High School
Hollywood, California

GLADYS KNIGHT

Gladys Knight
Class of 1961
Archer High School
Atlanta, Georgia

Varsity Basketball; Glee Club; Yearbook Staff;
Cheerleader; Student Council; Modern Dance.

"Pip"

ZOHRA LAMPERT

Zohra Lampert
Class of 1948
High School of Music and Art
New York, New York

SHARI LEWIS

Phyllis Hurwitz
Class of 1949
High School of Music and Art
New York, New York

"Pint size pirouette."

JOHN LINDSAY

John Vliet Lindsay
The Sixth Form of 1940
St. Paul's School
Concord, New Hampshire

President; Isthmian; Shattuck.

Yale.

ART LINKLETTER

Arthur Gordon Linkletter
Class of 1929
San Diego High School
San Diego, California

Timalathean 3, 4; Ex-Committee 4; Treasurer
Senior B 4; Senior A Cabinet 4; Class B
Basketball; Debate Team 4.

"Art"

"Take a trip around world."

44

ANITA LOOS

Anita Loos
Class of 1907
San Diego High School
San Diego, California

"My tongue within my lips I rein,
For who talks much talks in vain."

"The pen is mightier than the sword."

JOHNNY MATHIS

Johnny Mathis
Class of 1954
George Washington High School
San Francisco, California

Student Body President; Registry (Home
Room) President; Member of the Executive
Council; Swimming; Basketball; Music;
Basketball Team; Track Team.

San Francisco State

WALTER MATTHAU

Walter Matthow
Seward Park High School
New York, New York

President of Annex 22; Seward World; Folio
Staff; Track Team; Class Day Committee.

"Ripe in wisdom is he."

GOLDA MEIR

Goldie Mabowehz
Class of 1916
North Division High School
Milwaukee, Wisconsin

Elective Course, 3 yrs.; Lincoln Society;
Science Club; Pageant.

"Those about her
From her shall read the perfect ways of honor."

ROGER MILLER

Roger Miller
Class of 1953
Erick High School
Texola, Oklahoma

Traditions are observed!

YVETTE MIMIEUX

Gloria Mimieux
Class of 1961
Hollywood High School
Hollywood, California

CURTELL MOTTON

Curtell Motton
Class of 1958
Encinal High School
Alameda, California

A.S.E.H.S. President; Varsity Football;
California Scholarship Federation; Block E;
3A President; Varsity Basketball.

*"He will go places because
he has the ability to lead others."*

BESS MYERSON

Bess Myerson
Hunter High School
New York, New York

Music.

Laughter is everywhere!

JOE NAMATH

Joseph Willie Namath
Class of 1961
Beaver Falls Area High School
Beaver Falls, Pennsylvania

Audio-Visual Aids 11, 12; Knights of Safety 12;
Pep 10; Varsity Club 12; Baseball 11, 12;
Basketball J.V. 10, 11, 12; Football 10, 11, 12; Home
Room Secretary 10.

*"'Joe'...magician with a football
...always ready to have fun...carefree."*

PATRICIA NEAL

Patsy Neal
Class of 1943
Knoxville High School
Knoxville, Tennessee

RICK NELSON

Rick Nelson
Hollywood High School
Hollywood, California

*Tuna
Casserole*

JACK NICHOLSON

John Nicholson
Manasquan High School
Manasquan, New Jersey

Blue and Gray 1, 2, 4;
Rules Club President 1, 2; Football 1;
Basketball Manager 2; Study Club 3;
Junior Play 3; Table Tennis Club 3;
Senior Play 4; Class Vice-President 4.

Turkey!

KEN NORTON

Kenneth Norton
Class of 1961
Jacksonville High School
Jacksonville, Illinois

Football 1, 2, 3, 4; Basketball 1, 2, 3, 4;
Track 1, 2, 3, 4; Hi-Y.

*"And—what is more, you'll be
a Man, my son."*

TONY ORLANDO

Michael Anthony Orlando Cassivitis
New York, New York

ARNOLD PALMER

Arnold Daniel Palmer
Class of 1947
Latrobe High School
Latrobe, Pennsylvania

General..."Arnie" served on Student Service...
High Post reporter...appeared
in "Merchant of Venice"...four-year
golfer...Pennsylvania State Golf Champ.

GREGORY PECK

Eldred Gregory Peck
Class of 1933
San Diego High School
San Diego, California

Advanced Glee; Boys' Hi Jinx;
Class B Football; Interclass Baseball.
State

TONY PERKINS

Anthony Perkins
Class of 1950
Buckingham Browne and Nichols School
Cambridge, Massachusetts

Soccer 11; Tennis 11; Spectator Staff 11, 12;
Co-Literary Editor, Spectator 12;
Varsity Tennis 12; Glee Club 12.

When he entered B&N in the seventh grade, Anthony Perkins was the class magician. This year, he reestablished this reputation with his appalling, poker-faced demonstration of changing electricity to water at the Science Fair. Tony is a true musician in his own right. His desk always contains sheet music of some popular song, and at a recess time you will find him struggling with Pete White for positions on the piano bench. Members of the *Spectator* will always remember Tony for the original entertainment which he provides at evening *Spectator* meetings; members of French 4a will not soon forget his biting verbal battles with Mr. Kenney; and his close friends will miss his humorous stories, told over lemon and lime (with plain water) at Brighams.

JAMES PIKE

James Pike
Class of 1930
Hollywood High School
Hollywood, California

Annual 5, 6; League Debater; C.S.F;
Oratorical Winner

LEONTYNE PRICE

Leontyne Price
Laurel, Mississippi

BONNIE PRUDDEN

Bonnie Prudden
Class of 1933
Horace Mann School for Girls
New York, New York

*"There's a language in her eye,
her cheek, her lip,
nay her foot speaks."*

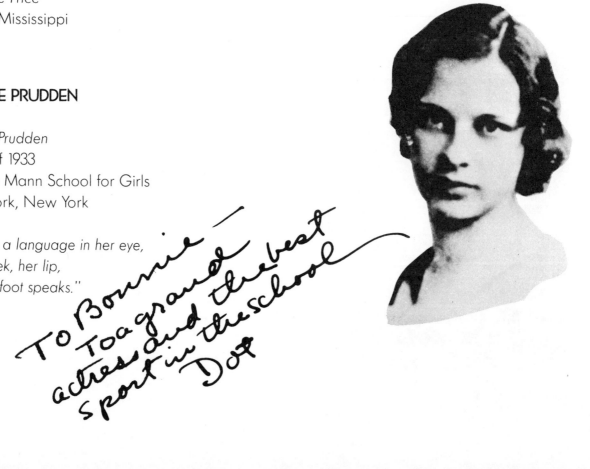

ROBERT REDFORD

Robert Redford
Class of 1954
Van Nuys High School
Van Nuys, California

JASON ROBARDS

Jason Robards II
Class of 1940
Hollywood High School
Hollywood, California

Captain Cross-Country Team; Journalist.

BROOKS ROBINSON

Brooks Robinson, Jr.
Class of 1955
Little Rock Central High School
Little Rock, Arkansas

Seniors have

PETE ROSE

Pete Rose
Class of 1960
Western Hills High School
Cincinnati, Ohio

fun together!

DIANA ROSS

Diana Ross
Cass Technical High School
Detroit, Michigan

JERRY RUBIN

Jerry Clyde Rubin
Class of 1956
Walnut Hills High School
Cincinnati, Ohio

Chatter 10-12; Sports Editor 11; Co-Ed 12;
Big Brothers' Peanuts; Student Council 12;
Programs Inc. 10; "Victoria Regina";
Sigma 9-12.

JANE RUSSELL

Jane Russell
Van Nuys High School
Van Nuys, California

JOHN SAXON

Carmen Orrico
New Utrecht High School
Brooklyn, New York

Ricky's ambition is to become an actor. He likes dressing well, physical culture, and girls. We're sure he'll be a great success on the stage or in the movies.

NEIL SEDAKA

Neil Sedaka
Lincoln High School
Brooklyn, New York

Music Honor Society; Supply Squad.

BOBBY SHORT

Robert Short
Class of 1941
Danville High School
Danville, Illinois

Triple A 2-4; A Cappella 3, 4; Maroon and
White 2-4; ''Moments Musical'' 3, 4.

I really can't say what I want to..

STEVE SMITH

Stephen Conant Smith
Class of 1962
Maine Township High School East
Park Ridge, Illinois

M Club 2, 3, 4, President 4; Maine Historical
Society 3, 4; Baseball 1; Basketball 1, 2, 3, 4;
Football 1, 2, 3, 4, Captain 4, Most Valuable
Player 4; Track 2, 3, 4; National Honor
Society 3, 4; Science Award 1.

DICK SMOTHERS

Dick Smothers
Verdugo Hills High School
Tujunga, California

so just don't forget me ...hey?

TOM SMOTHERS

Tom Smothers
Verdugo Hills High School
Tujunga, California

CARRIE SNODGRASS

Carrie Snodgrass
Class of 1963
Maine Township High School East
Park Ridge, Illinois

Biology Club 2; G.A.A. 1, 2; "Midsummer
Night's Dream" 4; Pep Club 1, 3; Stagecrafters'
Club 1, 2; Variety Show 1.

61

Loads of luck to a cute kid Edna

BRUCE SPRINGSTEEN

Bruce F. Springsteen
Class of 1967
Freehold High School
Freehold Boro, New Jersey

WILLIE STARGELL

Wilver Stargell
Class of 1958
Encinal High School
Alameda, California

J.V. Basketball; Varsity Basketball;
J.V. Baseball; Varsity Baseball;
Projection Club; J.V. Football.

"Let me sing until I 'flat' myself to death."

JIMMY STEWART

James Maitland Stewart
Class of 1928
Mercersburg Academy
Mercersburg, Pennsylvania

Marshall; Third Football Team, '24, '25, '26;
Track Squad, '26; Karux Board, '25,
Art Editor, '26, '27, '28; Marshall Orchestra, '28;
Choir, '28; Stony Batter Club, '28;
Class Day Committee, '28.

Venturing into a certain well-known room in Main you are likely to think you are interrupting the prologue of a miniature Roxy, for such is the disconcerting impression created by the moving strains of Jim's accordion and the bellowing efforts of his companions.

Nor is music "Jim's" only talent, for his skill in drawing has long been the pride of the Karux Board. In spite of Cicero's best attempts to overcome him, "Jim" is a good student and invariably comes out on top.

"Jim"   "Stew"   "Elmer"

Princeton

BILLY TAYLOR

William Edward Taylor, Jr.
Class of 1938
Dunbar High School
Washington, D.C.

Choral; Orchestra; Music.
To be a music arranger.

*"A boy whose popularity
Will never, never wane:
Because his love of harmony,
Will bring him lasting fame."*

DICK VAN DYKE

Dick Van Dyke
Danville High School
Danville, Illinois

NATALIE WOOD

Natalie Wood
Class of 1955
Van Nuys High School
Van Nuys, California

FARON YOUNG

Faron Young
Class of 1950
Fair Park High School
Shreveport, Louisiana

Football '48-'50; Boys' Glee Club '48;
Choir '48-'50.

Seniors say "Goodbye"!

Marian Anderson

ORGANIZATIONS

CALIFORNIA SCHOLARSHIP FEDERATION

First row: C. Jones, D. Magner, S. McElhinney, N. Ny, M. Nielsen, Y. Hunsaker, S. Kahn, J. Ianne, C. King, N. Kantzer, M. Lockheed, E. Morris.

Second row: N. Nardi, J. Horvitz, P. Kranz, A. Mango, M. Matlaf, J. Needman, M. Menges, K. Minkoff, K. Johnson, K. Hewitt, J. Mascolo, D. Halkides, G. Hunter.

Third row: K. Kofford, D. McComb, A. Holbrook, L. Noble, C. Heckler, J. Lulow, S. Hastings, N. Basaites, R. Major, C. Leo, R. Norman.

Fourth row: G. Liddle, R. Kaufman, **S. Keach,** G. Martin, J. Kahan, S. Kipperman, M. Lebowitz, E. Mezger, Y. Morris, D. Holt, M. Hollander.

Fifth row: I. Medall, H. Hacker, H. Hoffman, M. Blonsky, G. Newbauer.

SCHOLARSHIP CLUBS

Students with high grades compose the Van Nuys chapter of the California Scholarship Federation. Members enjoyed the C.S.F. play, "A Day of Broadcasting," in the fall semester and a picnic in the spring. In the fall the president was Commissioner of Scholarship Sarah Combs; succeeding her in both offices was Sparky Smith in the spring semester. Vice-presidents were Joel Shulman and Jody Ames.

STUDENT COUNCIL

CLASS OFFICERS, THIRD CLASS: **Israel Goldstein,** Secretary

First row: Jackie Haddon, Doreen Collett, Linda Fraser, Jeanine Tough, Lynne Carberry, Barb Sanvidge, Jane Maxwell.
Second row: Doug Arnett, Peder Neilson, Jane Halwa, Bob MacNair, Ursula Wirth, John Senst, Kelley Reynolds.
Third Row: Steve Burkhart, Alistair Saul, Rick Luckett, Erik Taynen, John Black, **Doug Henning.**

Arista and National Honor Society Officers

The National Honor Society came to Lincoln in 1958 with its unique induction, its scholarship fund, its community service projects. The founding officers—Gary Caplan, **Liz Holtzman,** Sheila White, John Markoff—and the advisors—Mrs. A. Clynch, Mrs. F. Kohn, Mrs. M. Heller—brought a dynamic organization to a dynamic school.

To some of you, Arista was an induction ceremony and a blue-and-gray pin; a reward for scholarship. To others, it was tutoring students in math and history, and implementation of scholarship.

Elizabeth Holtzman: second row, third from left.

EPHEBIANS

James Pike

EPHEBIAN SOCIETY

To become an Ephebian is the highest honor a student at Van Nuys High School can attain. The first Ephebians were a group of Greeks of outstanding leadership, scholarship, and character. The present-day Ephebian Society is carried on by students with the same distinctive qualities as those of the founders, plus a vital interest in civic affairs.

Each year the graduating class, in conjunction with the faculty, selects members to represent them in carrying out the aims of the society. Those who have achieved membership have not only been honored, but have been given opportunity to serve their fellowman and their community.

First row: Franchot, Bohlen, Harman.
Second row: Dent, Dole, Scully, O'Connor, Michalis, Tilghman,
D. Lindsay, H. Wheelwright, Mann.
Third row: F. Rockefeller, Bodine, **J. V. Lindsay,** Hurd.

REPRESENTATIVE COUNCIL

Representative council members and their alternates are elected from each second-period class to serve for one semester. Presiding over the monthly meetings were the Student Body Presidents. Sheryl King led the winter council, with Rich LeGassick following in the spring. Each member of the Board of Control is responsible for a table and for guiding the discussion when the group breaks up into smaller units. Some projects of the year were the Clean-Up Campaign and a discussion of the qualities needed for leadership. The council serves to unite the students of the school and the faculty.

THE G.O.

We will remember the transformation of the G.O. from a static figurehead to a dynamic, flexible student government. With the aid and guidance of Miss Pearl Crystal, the Holtzman twins, Bob and Liz, Bunny Greene, Susan Stein, and Joe Martori have succeeded in bringing to Lincoln a sing, a January graduation, student-faculty competitions, the free G.O. movie, the braille club, the year-long tenure of office... so many innovations which will become a part of Lincoln tradition. You may take pride in the fact that it was through your efforts that this G.O. was created, and through your support that it has been maintained.

Third row: John Starr, Seymour Rosenberg, **Gerald Ford,** William Schuiling, Clarke Vennemen, Leo Van Tassel, Roy Brown, James Johnston, Ralph Blocksma.

Annual Staff

Diana Gizir and **Carole Burnett** were two more of those faithful reporters who are so essential to the success of a paper.

Just as the planets, which provide undisputed astrological guidance for all of us, reflect the light of the sun, so does the colorful Hollywood High School News reflect the life of Hollywood High School.

The *News* this year has been responsible for several hundred cheerful dispositions and smiling faces every Tuesday noon, for the student body has enjoyed chuckling over such amusing and entertaining columns as "The Roving I" and "Reflections in the Mirror," beaming with pride while reading every well-written account of the latest sports events, and deliberating thoughtfully over such significant editorials as "Please Pardon Us, Miss Hollywood."

An energetic and enthusiastic group of reporters gave their best cooperation to the editors in the work that involves more diligence, patience, and industry than any other school activity. **Carole Burnett,** Blanche Capps, Marise Cherin, Diana Gizir, and Bob Parsons should be praised for their "on the spot coverage" of all the news-worthy events on the campus. They have been constantly on the job during school and have often donated many hours after school.

PLEIAD

First row: Haskell, Munro.
Second row: Kniffin, Horn, **Hammond,** Jeter, Werner (Editor), Browning, Parker, Theaman.

First row: Lorne Duncan, Lilian Sohn, Dorothy Zaretsky,
Manuel Shaw, Morton Parker, Isabel Fuller, Leonard Swallow,
Monte Halperin.
Second row: Roy Matas, Bernice Harrison, Nathan Goody,
Erwin Green, Beatrice Rogers, Tabala Sures, Israel Freedman,
Barney Bay, Sol Grand.

The 1928 Karux

First row: Sellery, Seabrook, **Stewart,** Rose, Coburn, Foothorap,
Gibbons.
Second row: Foulk, Swain, Bockes, Cochran, Huyett, Ball.
Third row: Mr. Barham, Loeb, Summerfeldt, Ullman, Meck, Mr. Tobey.

CLUBS

LINCOLN REPORT

The Lincoln Literary Society displayed its talent in the main assembly on Oct. 25. The program was exceptionally good and of great interest to all.   The program was entirely composed of suffragette numbers. Miss **Goldie Mabovitz** gave an original talk on the "Prospects of Women Votes."

The Lincoln Society cordially invites all students to attend its meetings and receive a free course in public speaking.

Pike, Green, Goldburg, Dunsmoor, Woodbury.

THE POND

It is sort of chilly down here at the pond. Little baby tadpoles are swimming under the thin ice. A woodpecker is at work not far from here, I can hear him pecking away. Sea-gulls are also around. I can hear them off in the distance. We are pretty far from the ocean so I'm wondering what the gulls are doing here. It sounds like a bird-farm around here. There are so many different birds. One bird is tweeting right above me. I'd better not look at him or he might fly away.

The cold wind is still blowing, stopping now and then. The dry weeds are wavering to its song. The whole forest is alive. Pretty soon the tadpoles will be swimming all around. The trees don't have any leaves yet, but soon they will turn green. The spring is here and the year starts its endless cycle.

I guess we do take this cycle for granted. And there is no reason why we should. But could you ever think of summer without a spring before? Or a fall without winter coming? If one of these seasons were left out what would you do? I don't know. But it is good it won't. We would get bored with one or two seasons every three hundred and sixty-five and a half days. While winter was around I used to think, "When will this ever end?" Well now it has, and maybe I'm sad that winter will never be here again. Oh sure, a new one will come but no new one can take the place of the old one. But these new ones will change to old ones. I wish the winter I used to love would return.

Arlo Guthrie '65
Symposium

ORATORICAL CONTEST

The International Oratorical Contest was won at Hollywood this year by **James Pike,** whose subject was "The Torch of Democracy." There was much interest evinced in the contest this year and six students were chosen for the semi-finals—Rollin Woodbury, Lawrence Dunsmoor, Joseph Costello, James Green, Helene Goldburg, and James Pike. In his oration James endeavored to show that it is our duty to uphold the ideals of our democracy as handed down to us by our forefathers and not to let outside forces undermine it. In the Times Semi-Finals James won over the major loop of city schools and placed third in the Pacific-Southwest Finals.

Neil Diamond: *top row, first on left.*

Blue Notes

Left to right: **Hammond,** Milling, Smadbeck, Theaman, Jeter,
LaFarge, Browning, Post, Reynolds, Clark, Munro, Gravlin, Kniffin.
Seated: Mr. Lessing.

Fifth row: J. Paterson, W. Kilgore, **W. Stargell,** R. Orem, D. Young, M. Auelua.

CHOIR PERFORMS

Encinal's Choir is a group of students carefully chosen from the vocal classes under the direction of Mr. Gaunt. The Choir has performed for school assemblies and various programs at Alameda's grammar schools. They attended the annual music clinic held at the College of the Pacific.

Bess Myerson: middle.

BAND, AND VOCAL

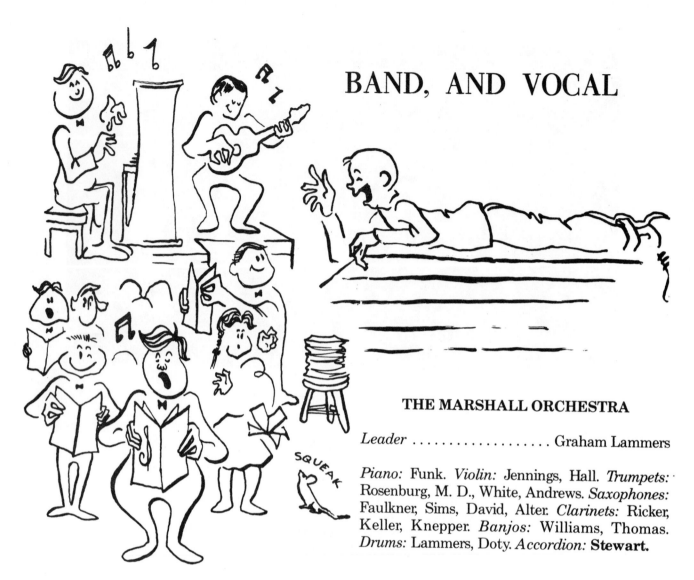

THE MARSHALL ORCHESTRA

Leader .... Graham Lammers

Piano: Funk. *Violin:* Jennings, Hall. *Trumpets:* Rosenburg, M. D., White, Andrews. *Saxophones:* Faulkner, Sims, David, Alter. *Clarinets:* Ricker, Keller, Knepper. *Banjos:* Williams, Thomas. *Drums:* Lammers, Doty. *Accordion:* **Stewart.**

"How irksome is this music to my heart."
Henry VI   (Act II, Scene I)

First row: **Stewart,** Faulkner, Sims, David, Alter, Lammers.

Fifth row: Lemon, Kirkbride, **Stewart,** Skillman, Flock, Hunt, Brown.

MUSIC HONOR SOCIETY

Neil Sedaka: second row, fourth from right.

"He Profits Most Who Serves Best"

To those activities which interest him, Youth gives unfailing service. Whether to country or to school, his devotion and loyalty are boundless.

SERVICE CLUBS

Third row: Hubbard, Levy, Chapman, Kenney, James, Gallenkamp, **Burnett,** Bonney, Drader, Jocelyn, Funke, Goode, Holt, LeVine, Lynch, Allan, Field.

AUDIO-VISUAL AIDS

Joe Namath: first row, first from right.

SCHOOL STORE

First row: **Hammond,** Post.
Second row: Haskell; Wales, Baker, Antell.

Fourth row: **B. Redford,** J. Dawson, R. Paolucci, K. Brown,
R. Nelson, J. Parmley, E. Tolmas, H. Allen, J. Quintana, C. Rendall, H.
Long.

SUPPLY SQUAD

Neil Sedaka: top row, second from left.

SOCIAL CLUBS

Second row: Kuri, **Kellerman,** Nilsson, Grant, Brown, Nance,
Romandy, Mallinson, Jaeger, Young, Bronston.

THE MISSIONARY SOCIETY

First row: Butler, L. T. Adamson, **J. V. Lindsay,** Dent, D. A. Lindsay,
P. B. Taylor, Geissler, Herrick, H. T. Hilliard, Henderson, Belding,
Cavanagh, A. R. Jones, G. P. Blake, C. T. Whitehouse, J. S. Smith,
P. Clark, Storer, Bucknall.

DRAMATIC CLUB

GOODBYE, MY FANCY

Agatha Reed	Judy Palmateer, Deanne Wagoner
Jim Merrill	Don Washbrook, Tom Albert
Matt Cole	**Stacy Keach,** Mike Richman
Grace Woods	Kim Ellis, Sharon Gibbs
Ellen Griswold	Pat McKinley, Tammy Burnham
Claude Griswold	Gail Johnson
Miss Shackleford	Julie Arthur, Carlie Zupp
Ginny Merrill	Marilyn Mason, Terry Pearlson
Mary Nell	Diane Hess, Ronnie Golden
Dr. Pitt	Louis Bencivenga, Bob Mercer
Miss Bradshaw	Hope Erlich, Brianne Surrey
Prof. Dingley	Mark Sollenberger, Mike Mahr

A Pageant of Thanksgiving to America

November The Twenty-fourth.
Orchestra.
EPISODES OF THE PAGEANT.

I.   The Spirit of Thanksgiving.
1   The Pilgrims.
2   The Declaration of Independence.
  II.   Interlude: Our Flag . . . . . Lincoln Society
    Betsy Ross . . . . **Goldie Maboweez**
    General Washington . . . . Hasso Pestalozzi
    Thomas Jefferson . . . . Ben Wiener
  Sewing Girls—Minnie Schostak, Irene Weber, Verna Shuler, Evelyn Hochschild, Ruth Matzek, Josephine Guzetta, Florence Ogle.
  Song—"The Star Spangled Banner"
    . . . . School
3   The Expansion of Our Nation.
  III.   Interlude: War.
4   A Crisis.
5   The Development of Our Nation.
    a. Invention.
    b. Immigration.
    c. Industry, agriculture, and education.
  IV.   Finale: Peace.
    Song—"America" . . . . School
  V.   Processional.

Stacy poses Marilyn for the picture for *Life.*

June Carter

The Ivory Door
A. A. Milne
CAST
PROLOGUE

King Hilary	Nancy Wertheimer
Prince Perivale	Betty West
Servant	Maxine Bluhm

THE PLAY

King Perivale	Anna Erskine
Brand (his body-servant)	Helene Levison
Anna	Belle Schloemer
Thora	Katherine Scherman
The Chancellor	Billie Palmer
Jessica	Virginia Schuyler
Anton	Elsie Rowe
Old Beppo	Dorothy Durning
Simeon	Deborah Hunt
Count Rollo	Isabel Tiefenthal
The Mummer	**Bonnie Prudden**
Titus	Cynthia Rose

SOLDIERS OF THE GUARD

Carlo	Marjorie Hunt
Bruno (Captain of the Guard)	Hildegarde Becher
Princess Lilia	Betty MacIver

A GLIMPSE OF THE FUTURE

The King	Margaret Williams
The Prince	Peggy Stern
Stage Manager	Barbara Girsdansky
Prompter	Maxine Bluhm

THE IVORY DOOR

Pictured above are the leading actors who will appear in "And Came the Spring." Shown, from left to right, are: Sara Brier, Mary Hinkamp, Charles Bean, Bill Robertson, **Patsy Neal,** David Lea, Katherine Stubley.

First row: Porter, **Stewart,** Foran, Hunt, Gordon, Corrigan, Waters.
Second row: King, Potts, Moyer, McLeod, Seabrook, Pryor, Oram, Chalfant.
Third row: Loeb, McCue, Kagen, Griswold, Coburn, Brown, Padgitt, Mr. Cass.

First row: Melvoin, Ayers, Bassett, **Heston,** Wolsey, DeLay (*sponsor*),
Dalstrom, Compere, Engelhard, Fisher, Rennacker.
Second row: Ward, Dawson, Borregaard, Bond, Gordon, Mark,
Buehler, Green, Barr, Meacham, Grauer, Stange, Strasser.

First row: T. Gherna, V. Reese, J. Holmes, E. Cummins, L. Adams.
Second row: H. McLain, E. McNamee, D. Hanson, B. Steely, **D. Van
Dyke,** S. Swisher, B. Shepard, J. Bell, L. Hahne, Miss M. Miller.
Third row: W. St. John, N. Noble, C. Whitesell, J. A. Guin, B. Kinney,
I. Miller, B. Dreher, E. Engle, P. Lauten, J. Linck.

MIDNIGHT LIBRO PROUDLY

DICK VAN DYKE

PRESENTS–

THE CAST

Samuel Hardman	Jack Selby
Claire Greenwood	Evelyn Cummins
Bob Morris	**Dick Van Dyke**
Mrs. Wick	Patricia Roark
Hugh Nichols	Leo Adams
Julia Greenwood	Virginia Reese Paula Ward
Ellen	Bobette Steeley
Leonard	Alan Taylor
Kate Bagley	Jane A. Guin
Eddie Bower	Fred Ackelmire
Joe Howard	Wayne St. John
Mr. Smith	Don Hanson
Wini Randall	
Coach	Miss Mary Miller
Stage Staff	Marian Karlstrom, Connie Winona
Sound Effects	Phil Johnson

Whitesell, Nancy Frankeberger, Winona Hopewell

Curtell Motton, halfback

Tommy Harper, quarterback

Alameda runner is stopped by **Curt Motton.**

Football

Third row: Coach Read, Coach Matula, M. Sherry,
N. Wallace, B. Brandenburger, D. Mitrick, F. Foster, A. Smith, P. Millet,
C. Harless, J. Hogan, B. Orem, M. Rexinger, T. Bowers, Head Coach
Marberry. *Second row:* K. Okubo, M. Watson, M. Jaramillo, W. King,
J. Lewis, J. Lennear, A. Guadalupe, V. Morelli, G. Gray, B. Rhoten,
D. Parslow, J. Ashley. *First row:* C. Hathaway (Mgr.), R. Williams,
R. Davis, F. Elmore, **T. Harper,** J. McCauley, D. Pinion, **C. Motton,**
Jean Kean, L. Branchaud, M. Mattingly (Mgr.).

Tom Harper makes good yardage against Alameda.

SENIOR TIGERS

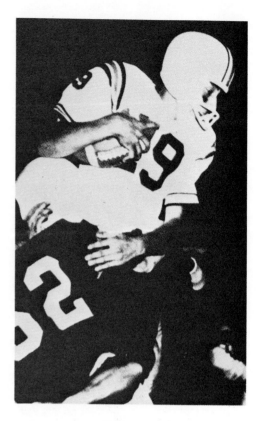

Joe Namath
All-State, ALL MAC, Quarterback

Joe Namath

First row: Cockfield, E., Pelaia, Jackson, Patterson, Kondracki,
Namath, Coach Bruno, Harris, Krzemienski,
Golmont, Heistand, Krivak, Seaburn.

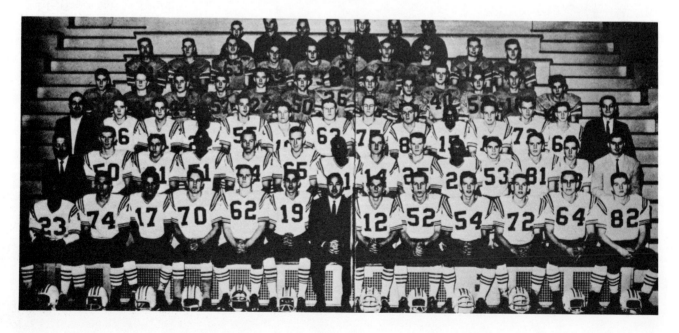

Ken Norton

ISTHMIAN FOOTBALL TEAM

Front row: Hays, Cox, Jessup, Brewster
Second row: **Lindsay, J.V.,** Redmond, Niedringhaus, Mechem,
Capt. Dent, Lindsay, D.A., Jones, A.B., Baker
Back row: Mr. Lloyd, Wheeler, Franchot, Treadwell, Taylor,
Townsend, Scully, Geissler, Willis, Hoyt

*Without,
the roar of football
victory booms.*

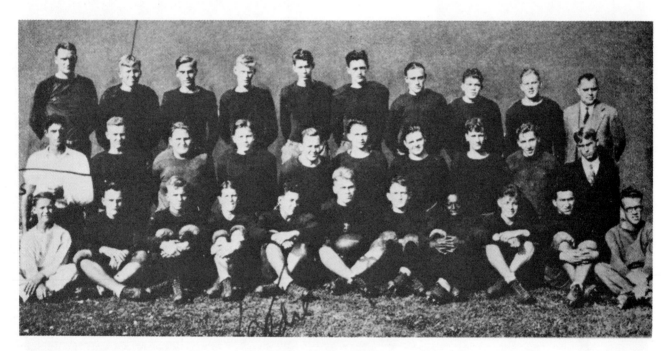

FIRST TEAM FOOTBALL

First row: Harold Bosscher, John Heinzelman, Louis Cooley, Allan Elliott, Ed Preston, **Gerald Ford,** Robert Matson, Silas McGee, Russell Koepnick, Michael Nassiff, Leo Van Tassel (Mgr.).
Second row: Leon Joslin, Russell Schipper, Wallace Smith, Harry Beall, Herbert Ross, LaVerne Knowles, Franklyn Clark, Ford Lipscomb, Marvin Blackport, Malcolm Elliott.
Third row: Coach Gettings, Robert Nelson, Floyd Thomas, Peter Dood, Milton Register, Jerry Bouman, Arthur Brown, Archie Ross, Richard Zylstra, Wickett (Mgr.).

Pete Rose, West Hi's shifty scatback, twists and turns his
way through three Hughes defenders on his way to a score.

BASEBALL

Wilver Stargell makes the long stretch at first.

Curtell Motton

Shortstop **Tom Harper** moves up to field grounder.

Varsity Baseball—Second row: E. Throckmorton (Mgr.),
G. Fenstermaker, M. Smith, **W. Stargell, T. Harper,** R. Davis, J. Lewis,
T. White, D. Oakes (Mgr.), B. Neuman (Mgr.). *First row:* J. Bownds,
M. Millet, M. Jaramillo, D. Pinion, **C. Motton,** F. Elmore.

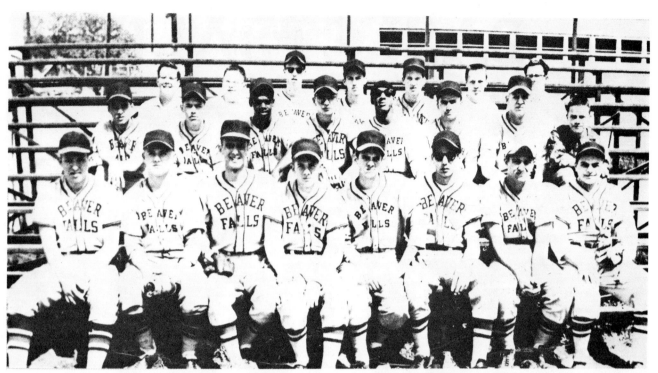

First row: R. Niedbala, Kondracki, Stevenson, Weaver, Gillingham, **Namath,** Pelaia, Betters.

Jimmy Hunter throws a curve.

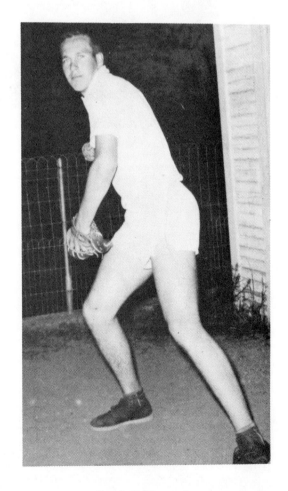

Brooks Robinson, Jr.

BASKETBALL

FAKE,

Joe Namath

SHOOT,

FOUL

Ken Norton

Left to right: Werner, Graves, Chernis, Mohan, LaFarge, Parker, **Hammond,** Glass, Milling, Mr. Kronholm (Coach), Cady, Wales, Clark, Gravlin, McKnight, Edwards, Horn (Mgr.).

The 1960 varsity basketball team, led by Captain Dave Milling and Coach Kronholm, scrimmaged the Wamogo High School before Christmas Vacation.

After vacation, the team played the Cornwall Boys' Club and lost 49-22. Hammond and LaFarge scored 13 and 9 points respectively. Against Barlow the hoopsters lost 70-26, with LaFarge and Cady scoring 7 apiece. Watkinson, Milford, and Barlow trounced the Blues in three successive games. In their last game the Marvels were defeated by Kingswood J. V. 42-29. **Hammond,** LaFarge, Cady, Wales, Parker, Clark, Edwards, and Glass assisted Captain Milling throughout the season. The J.V. team, led by Chernis and Mohan, won one of their four games.

Demons Gave Fans Basketball Thrills

BASKETBALL TEAM

First row: Dessen, Lipkowitz.
Second row: Mondros, Black (Captain), Calhoun.
Third row: Watson, Wattman.
Fourth row: McCloskey (Mgr.), Dr. Ker (Director of Athletics), Danzig,
Lewbart, **Gottlieb,** Mr. McCann (Advisor), Moish Ingber (Coach).

VARSITY SQUAD

First row: Jim Sponholtz, George Collins, Dave Petrick, John Hanson,
Larry Eichler, Jim Brown.
Second row: John Rudin (Mgr.), Len Diorio, Bill King, Jeff Jonswold,
Bob Kuntz, **Steve Smith,** Dick Johnson, Barry Kahan, Dale Litney,
Bill Sprague (Mgr.).

TRACK

Cee Track: The Cees enjoyed one of their most successful seasons
and were beaten only by San Fernando and Van Nuys.
Outstanding performers were: Haskell O'Brien, Bob Jackson, Dan
Roark, **Tom Smothers,** Fred Sanchez, and Dick Wilenken.

First row: Wes Coulter, Jim Henderson, Gary Spangenberg, Jim
Hurst, Claude Young, Mr. Rosenberger (Coach), **Ken Norton**
(Co-captain), Bill Stanford, Malcolm Portee, Jack Ricks,
Tom Dailey.

First row: Ezmerlian, Soloman, **Robards,** Hemberger, Gaynor.
Second row: Argo, Vitto, Gage, Rodriguez, Ward.
Third row: Brown, Boughton, Menard.

Cross-Country

The cross-country team whose twofold duty it is to keep knotting muscles and stiffening legs in shape for the spring track season, and also to keep grid fans interested in something besides the Good Humor salesman during halftime periods this year, accomplished both these duties most adequately.

Under the seasoned eye of coach Merrill Bailey, the team this year was composed of Captain **Jason Robards,** ace distance man, Tom Argo, Jim Menard, Herrick Ward, Dave Rodriguez, and Arnold Soloman.

The cross-country team consisting of twenty-one boys was a pleasant surprise. This was the first year Oakville had seriously entered cross-country competition, and the team finished first at Zone 1 S.O.S.S.A. and placed fifth at S.O.S.S.A. Mike Carberry and Bob Legge finished second in their divisions, while **Doug Henning** was third in his.

First row: **Doug Henning,** John Fitzpatrick, Tim Parker, Bill Parker, Peter Zuloff, Ken Anderson, Murray Yewer.
Second row: Ron Krush, Ian Blakelock, Roger White, Doug Inkster, Mike Carberry, Bob Legge, Marc Couse, Peter Milne, Ed Newport.
Third row: Adrian Cianfrone.

Swimming

Julius La Rosa: top row, fourth from right.

Fencing

Under the guidance of Mr. S. Shapiro, the 1957-58 fencing team has attained the coveted top berth in the city, despite the oppressive competition of arch-rival Stuyvesant. Captain Herb Cohen has won over one hundred bouts in his P.S.A.L. career, setting a Lincoln record. June will find the team, devoid of Cohen, Co-captain Hal Krebs, Phil Rappaport, Sol Needle, and **Neil Diamond,** left with a slim chance of repeating this year's success.

Neil Diamond: second from right.

TENNIS

Althea Gibson

Mr. Tilden, Boutourline (Captain), Hayes, Mason, Mann, Lubets,
Perkins, Davis, Baty, MacStravic, Tyler, Sharmat, Wetherell (Mgr.).

Crewing

THE S.P.S. CREW

First row: O'Connor, W. G. Moore.
Second row: Sefton, J. S. Smith, A. R. Jones, Peabody, Fox.
Third row: Michalis, Harman, Tilghman, **J. Lindsay.**

Team captain and national junior champion **Clark Graebner** receives his hard-earned award from Mayor Celeste.

GOLF

Arnie Palmer set a mark for future Latrobe High School linksmen as he captured the W.P.I.A.L. golf crown and then journeyed to Penn State to win the state championship for the second straight year. Palmer set two new records, one by being the only boy ever to win the double crown twice, and the other by shooting the lowest score ever fired in the P.I.A.A. championship playoff. Palmer gained national recognition last summer when he qualified for the National Junior Open at Pittsburgh. He traveled to Detroit and fought his way to the final match, only to lose to Mac Hunter of California. Arnie is rated the number two junior golfer of the nation.

Led by Arnie Palmer, the golf squad coached by Mr. William Yates repeated as section champions for the fourth consecutive year. At the end of the regular season Latrobe tied with Greensburg for the first place, but won the rubber match for the crown. The linksmen then went on to the W.P.I.A.L. tournament only to lose in the semi-finals against Baldwin High School.

From the 1943 Milestone a month-by-month account of the academic year by Johnny Carson

I, *John Carson*, being of sound mind and body (this statement is likely to be challenged by my draft board and the high school faculty), deem it advisable to give you the lowlights of 1942 and 1943.

I can visualize 20 years from now when you sit down by the radio (listening to Roosevelt), with the old 1943 *Milestone* in your trembling hands, and as you glance over those remembrances, you will say to your son—"I wish I could get hold of that *?%") ¢/ *Milestone* staff." And then your little son will look at the *Milestone* and say meekly—"Hey, does this stink!"

Be that as it may, I have hereunto set my hand to the task of giving you a month by month, drip by drip, account of Norfolk High School activity during the year. If you like this account, tell my friends. (My friends include my mother, and others who have asked that their names be withheld.)

SEPTEMBER

As it goes without saying, school was opened this month and students looked with eager pleasure on an exciting and studious school year.

The first few hours in school were of course trying and nerve-racking, and general confusion reigned, but I am happy to say no lives were lost, although one freshman ended up in the furnace room instead of 209—which wasn't so bad when you consider the odds.

This month cowboy boots seemed to take the spotlight. There were so many boots around school, we got an offer from Republic Studio! Personally, I like the West, where men are men and women are women, but it's hard to tell which!

Football season opened this month and I went out to make the team. I would have made good if they hadn't found where I hid my brass knuckles!

Gosh! I wonder if you'll be in my homeroom again, stuck on the third floor.

OCTOBER

October was a big month for the Seniors. At the end of the month, they had so much money in their treasury, the faculty members received their back pay, and Mr. Gerdes had enough to pay his income tax!

The scrap drive was a big affair; it was "friendly rivalry" between the classes. "Friendly rivalry"—that's an old Spanish term meaning "Get your hands off our scrap pile before we break your arm." However, the Seniors collected everything except the janitor's jumper in their pile, and won the contest.

During the Hare and Hound race, the Seniors threw the Juniors off the trail. In fact they were so far off the trail, it was the only time a Junior Class came back on the bus from Omaha! But they finally arrived at the Norfolk golf course, the Seniors' hiding place. They were so late in getting there, they had to get off the fairway to let the Sunday morning golfers go by!

NOVEMBER

November was the month when everyone got the bird, and I certainly got it!

This month made all the students very war conscious, with black-outs, etc. In fact, this was one of the few months the students were even awake! All the students enjoyed the blackouts very much. They liked them so well, four unidentified senior boys attempted to put the power plant out of commission.

Gas rationing went into effect, and all the students took it in good spirit—it said in the paper. The limit was four gallons of gas a week, the police told Dan Hoion, when they saw him with a rubber hose in Mr. Burkhardt's gas tank! The football team ended a swell season at Columbus with Al Mather leading the scoring. Mather was arrested for exceeding the thirty-five-mile-an-hour speed limit (on an end run).

Johnny Carson: third row, fourth from left.

Cheers

WASH 'EM OUT
Wash 'em out ring 'em out
Hang 'em on the line
We can beat (other team) any old time.
Pull 'em in lay 'em out
Roll 'em up tight
Come on Cliffside fight, fight, fight.

RAH, RAH, REY, REY
Rah, rah, rey, rey, hip, hip, hey, hey
Rah, rey, hip, hey—hallabuloo Cliffside.

GIVE THEM A FIGHT
Give 'em a fight—Give 'em a scare
Cliffside tigers take a dare
Come on six come on seven
Come on Cliffside High Eleven.

C-L-I (clap, clap)
C L I (clap, clap) C-L-I (clap, clap)
C-L-I-F-F-S-I-D-E
C L I (clap, clap) C-L-I (clap, clap)
C-L-I-F-F-S-I-D-E
For the Red (clap, clap)
For the Black (clap, clap)
For the Red and Black we'll fight right
    back
For the Red (clap, clap)
For the Black (clap, clap)
For the Red and Black we'll fight right
    back.

VICTORY
Rah, rah, rie, Never say die,
V-I-C-T-O-R-Y
Treat 'em rough, why be tame?
Come on Cliffside take this game.

CL CL
CL CL CLIF IF IF IFSI SI SI SIDE
CLI double F side Park
CLI double F side Park
Team, team, team.

1-2-3-4
1-2-3-4   3-2-1-4
Who for? Why for?
Who ya' going cheer for
Cliffside, Cliffside
Team, team, team.

DRUMS
Drums, drums, drums, drums, drums
Drums, drums, drums, drums, drums
Drums, drums, drums, drums, drums
With a T with an E with a loud AM
With a T with an E with a loud AM
With a soft T E with a loud A M
With a T E A M yea team—team, team,
    team
Drums, drums, drums, drums, drums
Drums, drums, drums, drums, drums
Drums, drums, drums, drums, drums
Yea — Cliffside.

DECEMBER

The Juniors presented their play this month, and it was well received. The receipts were also well received by the Junior Class. I wouldn't say the Junior treasury was very low, but the Junior sponsor was seen three times at the Central Finance Company!

The faculty held their annual Christmas party this month, with Miss Walker dealing the cards. Mr. Gerdes played Santa Claus, and would have gotten away with it if he hadn't had his ninth-period book with him.

It was announced this month that the faculty basketball team would play the junior college Blackhawks. All insurance companies immediately cancelled the faculty members' policies! This month ended with Bob Jesson waiting at his fireplace with a club for Santa Claus and bag. Bob was interested in the bag, I believe.

JANUARY

A new year brings new classes, new tests, new faces, but the same old teacher! (The only way I'll get out of school now is to be drafted.) This is the month everyone progresses a half-year and becomes a little smarter—I tried explaining to the faculty!

Ward Moore suffered the only real setback, progressing rapidly backwards a half-year in boys' cooking class. They found Ward rolling around on the floor one day because the recipe said to roll in cracker crumbs! I wouldn't say Ward's cookies were very hard, but Larry Skalowsky ran over one of them and blew out two tires!

At this time I would like to say something about the semester tests, but they were afraid the administration might read the *Milestone*, so they wouldn't print it! (Fine chance the administration will read this.)

The month ended with students drooling icicles on the way to school!

FEBRUARY

Month of Washington's birthday. If Washington (who never told a lie) could hear some of the excuses the kids hand Mr. Gerdes every morning, he would turn over in his grave and get up and run for a third term—and probably say, "What, Roosevelt still in?"

Everyone was getting his date to the Junior-Senior banquet. For the benefit of the Sophomores, I will explain in detail how to get a date. The first thing to do is to call up the best-looking girl in school and ask her. After that, call up someone who will go with you! I was turned down so many times, I felt like a bed spread!

Not to mention the Valentine verse I received from my draft board which went like this: "Upon this February morn the draft board wishes to inform, we love you much, and all that stew, but never mind, we'll wait for you!"

MARCH

This month found students framing excuses to leave this beautiful and inspiring institution of learning to attend the basketball tournament work—they told Dean Wetzel as they caught him sneaking out the back door! The teachers, of course, stayed with the remaining students—Mr. Burkhardt informed Mr. Rohn, who was right behind Dean!

The music clinic was held this month and was a great success. Some unidentified magician gave a performance the same night, and was chased out of town.

Several of the boys who worked in war plants a few days, and a few of the teachers, had to pay income taxes on the 15th.

The March winds lived up to their reputation by blowing as hard as usual, with Johnny Ryan running a close second!

Dick Van Dyke

APRIL

April is the time of year when everyone begins to feel stronger, and to recuperate after the winter season. You could tell the teachers were getting stronger. They seemed to throw you out of class harder.

Les France started a commando course designed to toughen you up for the armed forces. He came to school on crutches the next day. (Honest!)

At this time of year, students engage in such activities as track meets, skipping school, class play, skipping school, *Milestone* work, skipping school, and others which include (this will kill you) skipping school!

Junior-Senior field day was held this month, and the boys enjoyed playing such childish games as drop the body, ring around the graveyard, etc. (Any bodies left over thirty days became property of the park management!)

Field Day

MAY

The school year is about to come to a close (and so is this stuff). As you sit reading this gift to the literary world, you will remember Sup't. Burkhardt's praise on the book in his message. Of course, this has nothing to do with the fact that no one had yet seen the book, including the superintendent!

Those of you who failed to make known your observance of Mr. McIntyre's birthday this month may still save face by bringing goodies and sweetmeats to the publications room.

The Senior Class play drew a large crowd recently, and the cast is in line for congratulations for presenting a swell play.

Graduation exercises are about the last activity on the school program, and they are being eagerly looked forward to.

Having been recognized as the epitome of success during my four years (so far) in Norfolk High School, I have been asked to jot down some of my secrets of getting along with the teachers. I oblige with the following:

1. Always hand in daily papers.
2. Laugh at the teacher's jokes.
3. Do an abundance of extra-credit work.
4. Laugh at the teacher's jokes.
5. Never chew gum during classes.
6. Laugh at the teacher's jokes.

(Numbers 1, 3, and 5 may be omitted and no appreciable difference will be noticed!)

Below is a list of the graduating Seniors of '43 who, during the course of the four years they have been confined here, never cheated in a test, never received a ninth period, and never perpetrated dastardly deeds in their minds concerning the bodily welfare of the faculty:

There are some rewards in making a yearbook (although it doesn't look as if we were working for any). A rather unexpected reward for the staff was a beautiful (and also good) chicken dinner a la carte. "A la carte"—that means for another dime we wash the dishes! I say the dinner was unexpected because of the money shortage that seemed to exist some place in the advertising department. This difficulty was cleared up at the dinner when Phillips tipped the waitress fifty dollars. (This aroused suspicion in the sponsor's mind.)

The sponsor was presented a gift by the group, which came as another surprise, being the economical group the staff is! (Phillips volunteered to pay for the gift—and rightly so!)

It is hoped that the *Milestone* staffs of years to come work as hard and as diligently and sell as many ads and books as this staff, so that they too will be able to have a dinner in their honor.

A recent survey of student opinion, conducted by a reliable sort of person, reveals the following results:

Most scholarly student: Gerald Faubol—He always wants to stay nine periods instead of the usual eight.

Best-looking boy: *John Carson*—(no comment).

Least likely to succeed: John—It is rumored that John was born with an egg-shaped head, and it is beginning to hatch!

Most athletic boy: *John Carson*—(no comment).

Why a chicken crossed the street: Because she sees Bob coming.

NIGHT BEFORE THE PROM
By Elliot Friedman (With Apologies)

'Twas the night before the prom, when all through the school
No one was studying, ignoring each rule;
The gym was fixed up with decorations galore,
Waiting for the kids that all this was for.
The fellows were dressed for three hours before,
But the girls kept them waiting all the while more,
And I in my tux, and she in her gown,
Had just started away for the ride into town,
When from back of my car there arose such a noise
I sprang from my car, but 'twas only the boys.
"Hello Bernie, Hiya Alvin, hail to you Lom,
I see that you kids are on your way to the prom.
We'll follow along and we'll get there O.K.
Oh have you seen Ira, by the way?"
We finally got there and started to jive,
When Ira tapped me and asked me for five.
When the hour of twelve began to tick,
We all upt and left with the girl of our pick,
And to top it all off, right in the hall,
We decided, school's not so bad after all.

THE SENIOR PROM

Roll up the curtain! Play again the wonderful act! Laugh, oh you happy ones! Glide to that ecstatic refrain! Love, see life, know joy! Join in the revelry of youth. Who dares say it has fled? Oh, play! Play again that romantic episode. Summon Memory. Unfold again the panorama of that happy night. Roll up that curtain, the gorgeous, golden curtain…roll…roll…roll.

It was a January evening in the early '30's. Hesitantly the moon was peeping and creeping from behind a cloud. Within, blithe, happy adolescence danced and laughed. The dance class protégés were crowning their teacher's hopes with success, for grace reigned supreme. What was that new strange look, that indefinable gaze in the depths of that lad's eyes? Why his quaking, "like a sighing furnace"? Why did he constantly stare in one direction? Why did he swallow and look so seriously lost in a labyrinth of thoughts? Why such deep and ponderous meditation on this, his happy prom night?

That girl—why did she list' so intently to those well, well-known strains as though they were some yet unheard notes, newly and harmoniously emitted from 'Apollo's lute"? Ah!

Then he spake. "Dear heart," he was saying, "let us go—let us go out there where we may be alone in the moonlight, alone with our thoughts and our love."

Then spake she. "Oh, John, surely no one would leave this class gathering. Surely no one would leave such gaiety. But we, dear, we are different. Nothing but our love could make us go. Come."

So they went. And the moon still peeped from behind the cloud. And 'way up there the moon laughed in sheer glee, for below they were in the moonlight—alone with their thoughts and their love—with fifteen or sixteen other couples—also alone.

The last act is over. Remembrances linger and memory holds sway. How often shall we again want to remember that rollicking dance, that last undergraduate social gathering 'way, 'way back in the '30's? How often shall we summon Memory? Soon our hearts will thrill, will skip a beat as we again watch that gorgeous, golden curtain roll…roll…roll.

Tony Perkins

Joe Namath, left.

Queen and Court

Stacy Keach

Joe Namath

And now for home...

Senior Celebs and Favorites

Friendliest Boy: Jerry D'Alessio; Friendliest Girl: Rita Boskin; Boy Comedian: **Leonard Hacker;** Girl Comedienne: Beverly Wexler; Boy Jitterbug: Herbert Rausher.

SUPERLATIVES

All Around Girl: Claire Comerford; All Around Boy: **Curt Motton;**
Girl Most Likely to Succeed: Edna Washington; Boy Most Likely to
Succeed: Jim Snider; Best Actress: Carmen Cutting; Best Looking
Girl: Linda Stone; Best Looking Boy: Leonard Palomino; Best Athlete:
Tom Harper; Girl Class Clown: Marilynne Purbeck; Boy Class
Clown: Gil Gray.

Senior Class Will

Abel—leaves her medal to Debby Ward

Baker—leaves her position on the health panel to anyone who is brave enough to take it

Beckers—leaves his charley horse to Connett

Berger—leaves her lederhosen to Dr. Rist

Bland—leaves this stuff to any fool who'll take it

Borders—leaves his collegiate clothes to Jim Baird

Calkins—leaves his razor to Wotka

Clark—leaves Jones as the last of the eternal quadrangle

Conzelman—leaves his long hair to a barber

Corrington—leaves his bright yellow pants to Biddle

Cranston—won't leave her sunlamp

Cullenbine—leaves coaching to Greensfelder

Cunningham—leaves her six-inch heels to Wehmiller

Depping—leaves her hair to Colleen

Dimmitt—leaves her indifference to Foote

Engle—leaves the eighth-grade girls to the cradle

Esserman—leaves his language to Townsend

Estep—can't spare anything

Gerlach—leaves his truck "broken down" in the parking lot

Greve—leaves "Greetings" to Blythe Cunningham

Gutman—leaves his curly hair to Bill Hassett

Guy—leaves all family cars to Steve

Hammond—wills his folk records to Mr. Lessing

Hardcastle—leaves her lucky charms to Mr. Eiseman

Harding—leaves his football pants

Hardy—leaves German vocabulary to Wotka

Harford—leaves rusty old fingernails to Keiffer

Harrison—leaves her ducktail to Dave Horner

Haven—leaves the hotdogs in physics to anybody who can eat them

Hein—leaves the beloved 'A' Varsity Basketball to Dubie

Herbst—leaves ten pounds to Connett

Hockaday—leaves her hips to Sutter

Idol—leaves his boldness to McCarthy

Jackes—leaves everything everywhere

Jordan—leaves his tricycle to Connett for better transportation

King—leaves Kay to the Junior boys

Langenberg—leaves his biology drag to Mark Weil

Levy—leaves his gum supply to whomever will take it

Magidson—leaves his used flash bulbs to the eighth-grade girls

McCarroll—leaves to concentrate on MEN

McDonald—leaves English class for the last time

McGinley—leaves R.B. to Sheila

McHaney—leaves her laugh

Metcalfe—wouldn't leave his car for anything

Moran—leaves the garage for the next sneaky people

Morrin—leaves 15-yard penalties to Meyer

Murphy—leaves catching to whoever wants it

Perkins—leaves a drawer full of dirty test tubes to "Doc" Walters

Rist, A.—leaves the fire escape to whoever gets there first

Rist, C.—leaves red hair, freckles, and pitching to Mike Lane

Rogers—leaves her ears to Don Hobbs

Ross—leaves his uniform to Gary Giessow

Ruwitch—leaves a good car to Bobby Bean

Schneeberger—keeps trying to leave

Scholz—leaves her blond hair to Buckley

Seddon—leaves the library to Miss Rutledge

Stocker—leaves his nicknames

Straub—all the promised advertisers to next year's persuasion

Terry—leaves the nags to Limo

Thieme—leaves Mr. Eiseman in tears

Wallas—leaves the stage to Kay Comfort

Wattenberg—leaves white pennies to time

Weidemueller—leaves to replace his car

Wulff—leaves Pat to Eric

Always Seen

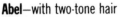

Abel—with two-tone hair
Baker—chewing gum
Beckers—limping
Berger—with the boys
Bland—bitter
Borders—writing in cement
Calkins—dropping passes
Clark—panicking when it rains
Conzelman—being unobtrusive
Corrington—fit to Kill'er
Cranston—with something missing
Cullenbine—running Burroughs
Cunningham—making blunders
Depping—bunny-hopping on Eades Bridge
Dimmitt—being sympathetic
Engle—flirting
Esserman—looking for "Band of Gold"
Estep—hot-rodding
Gerlach—exhibiting his pot
Greve—pulling the Review through
Gutman—making 27 points a game
Guy—at Page's
Haase—at Daisy dinner parties
Hardcastle—being nice
Harding—being cautious
Hardy—playing hypo
Harford—at home with C.G.
Harrison—knitting
Haven—with all A's
Hein—stalled at Steak 'n Shake in the jitney-bus
Herbst—changing her mind
Hockaday—stepping on her hockey stick

Idol—bitter
Jackes—being flustered
Jordan—working on cars
King—being simple
Langenberg—open-mouthed
Levy—talking
Magidson—in a hurry
McCarroll—looking neat
McDonald—in the bathtub
McGinley—wearing sweaters
McHaney—emotionally
Metcalfe—in a new Ford
Moran—looking tough
Morrin—in a tourney
Murphy—with Chip
Pflager—blitzed
Rist, A.—doing her algebra
Rist, C.—heading the World
Rogers—confused
Ross—late to school
Ruwitch—eating
Schneeberger—dodging girls
Scholz—hanging around the physics lab
Seddon—with Hoff
Stocker—going to Meyers
Straub—barely seeing
Terry—at 52 Middlesex
Thieme—using her hands
Wallas—bouncing
Wattenberg—with a Pepsi
Weidemueller—hunting
Wulff—with Murphy

Pet Peeves

Abel—clay pits
Baker—a person when he is always late
Beckers—Steak 'n Shake car hops
Berger—people who kiss me (in my family, that is)
Bland—being slugged, hit, pushed, slapped, tickled…
Borders—U. City Traffic Court
Calkins—dressing up
Clark—convertibles
Conzelman—people with inferiority complexes
Corrington—showers that suddenly scald you
Cranston—Knollwood Courts
Cullenbine—people who won't listen quietly to "Seven Dreams"
Cunningham—"squares"
Depping—people who want to cut my hair
Dimmitt—hamburgers without pickles
Engle—Straub's prices
Esserman—all people with pull
Estep—slow cars
Gerlach—people who don't come to soccer games
Greve—perverse people
Gutman—having his license suspended
Guy—the pixie who turns the hands of the clock at the drive-ins
Haase—smoke in the car
Hardcastle—procrastinators
Harding—a royal straight flush in Low Ball
Hardy—playing soccer in slush
Harford—"Herdy Herf"
Harrison—people who "know" how to play bridge
Haven—rhythm and blues
Hein—getting behind old cronies who drive 10 m.p.h.
Herbst—dogs
Hockaday—Martha

Idol—people who get cut easily
Jackes—sneaky people
Jordan—the beat-up track
King—girls that say they flunked a test and get an "A"
Langenberg—Freshman girls
Levy—Daddy-O
Magidson—flash bulbs
McCarroll—Ft. Lauderdale girls
McDonald—Nancy when she's mad
McGinley—"long hair" music
McHaney—turtle
Metcalfe—people who think Chevys are better than Fords
Moran—Jody
Morrin—dirty football
Murphy—talkative Al
Pflager—anything cheap
Rist, A.—having her picture taken
Rist, C.—going over 30 (m.p.h.)
Rogers—ice cube trays
Ross—Nelson Burton
Ruwitch—Connett
Schneeberger—curve balls
Scholz—people who think I bleach my hair
Seddon—looking for erasers
Stocker—Angus
Straub—Engle's empty billfold
Terry—Florida Racing Commission
Thieme—"the poor working girl"
Wallas—television commercials
Wattenberg—women drivers
Weidemueller—game wardens
Wulff—respectable ice boxes

Hey Chicko! *Don't panic!* *Let 'er rip!* *I'm dizzy!* *Ugh!* *Get hep!* *Always Heard* *Oh Romeo!* *Hubba, Hubba!*

Abel—"Let 'er rip, Lee!"
Baker—"Here now, I don't understand"
Beckers—"I'm dizzy"
Berger—"Why Hoff?"
Bland—"I have a question"
Borders—"Hi, Mr. Arnold"
Calkins—"Huh?"
Clark—"Eek, that animal!"
Conzelman—copying people
Corrington—"Bl-bl-bl-bl-blast i-i-i-it"
Cranston—"Let's get hep, gang"
Cullenbine—"Let's serious up"
Cunningham—"I'm sorry I'm late, but..."
Depping—giving her point of view?
Dimmitt—"Oh, Romeo..."
Engle—flattering girls
Esserman—"Aww, misdeal"
Estep—"You're rocking with the 'T'"
Gerlach—"Garge, you shunt"
Greve—"Vale"
Gutman—cutting
Guy—"Ugh"
Haase—"I thought I'd flunked"
Hardcastle—"Oh my!"
Harding—"The rules say..."
Hardy—"Doc, I got a pain"
Harford—"When I was on the Delta Queen..."
Harrison—"I'm going to have a party"
Haven—pickin' the cello
Hein—"Where at?"
Herbst—"Oh, you all..."
Hockaday—"Hey Lane, I got an A too"

Idol—being tactful?
Jackes—"God save the Queen!"
Jordan—getting mad
King—"When I grow up..."
Langenberg—"Don't push the panic button"
Levy—"I hope I didn't disturb you"
Magidson—"Have you done your informal?"
McCarroll—"What're you going to wear?"
McDonald—"Hoy"
McGinley—"But I didn't know..."
McHaney—"It's not me, it's my car"
Metcalfe—"Officer, MY name is Metcalfe"
Moran—arguing with Jody
Morrin—"Red dog"
Murphy—"No football this year"
Pflager—"Sogreat"
Rist, A.—trying to get the girls to pay attention in advisory
Rist, C.—making puns
Rogers—giggling
Ross—wheezing
Ruwitch—"The motion has been laid on the table"
Schneeberger—at the Indianapolis Speedway
Scholz—"Well, I know my sister's friends"
Seddon—"Well, because..."
Stocker—"Get me a turnkey"
Straub—"When I was at Kirkwood..."
Terry—reciting statistics
Thieme—"I think so"
Wallas—"Sorry, can't waste the gas"
Wattenberg—singing 3rd bass in chorus
Weidemueller—rarely
Wulff—"Hey, Chicko"

Heartbreak Hotel

The Continental   *Great Pretender*   *My Funny Valentine*   *Speedo*

Favorite Song

Night Train

Abel—Lover, Come Back to Me
Baker—Johnny
Beckers—Great Pretender
Berger—Long, Tall Sally
Bland—Just My Bill
Borders—It's a Big, Wide, Wonderful World
Calkins—If You Knew Susie
Clark—How Come You Do Me Like You Do, Do, Do
Conzelman—Stumbling
Corrington—Why Do Fools Fall in Love?
Cranston—Summertime
Cullenbine—Little Brown Jug
Cunningham—my variations of Beethoven's 6th Symphony
Depping—Heartbreak Hotel
Dimmitt—If I Loved You
Engle—The Continental
Esserman—Band of Gold
Estep—Work with Me, Annie
Gerlach—Don't Step on My Blue Suede Shoes
Greve—Don't Roll Those Blood-shot Eyes at Me
Gutman—Yes Sir, That's My Baby
Guy—Night Train
Haase—You Gotta Be a Football Hero
Hardcastle—I Wanta Be Evil
Harding—Daddy-O
Hardy—Living Around
Harford—Fling Hill Special
Harrison—My Funny Valentine
Haven—Salty Dog
Hein—Hands Off
Herbst—Heart and Soul
Hockaday—What Is a Boy?

Idol—Redhead
Jackes—My Lean Baby
Jordan—Rock Around the Clock
King—Speedo
Langenberg—Love for Sale
Levy—Love for Sale
Magidson—Victory at Sea
McCarroll—Moments to Remember
McDonald—Nancy with the Light Green Eyes
McGinley—Cross Over the Bridge
McHaney—Smokey Joe's Cafe
Metcalfe—Too Late
Moran—Run, Jody, Run
Morrin—No Money Down
Murphy—Why Do Fools Fall in Love?
Pflager—Tropical Heat Wave (Marilyn Monroe)
Rist, A.—Love and Marriage
Rist, C.—Sandpaper Ballet
Rogers—Black Denim Trousers
Ross—Moon over Miami
Ruwitch—Love Is a Many-Splendored Thing
Schneeberger—How Important Can It Be?
Scholz—I'll See You Again
Seddon—All Right, O.K., You Win
Stocker—anything white
Straub—Willie Can
Terry—Carolina Moon
Thieme—This Is a Husband?
Wallas—Tutti Frutti
Wattenberg—Hey Brother, Pour the Wine
Weidemueller—House of Blue Lights
Wulff—Lonesome Polecat

Favorite Movie

Abel—One Summer of Happiness
Baker—Love Me or Leave Me
Beckers—The High and the Mighty
Berger—Mr. McGoo
Bland—I'll Cry Tomorrow
Borders—Blackboard Jungle
Calkins—Susan Slept Here
Clark—One Desire
Conzelman—East of Eden
Corrington—The Killer's Loose
Cranston—Picnic
Cullenbine—All That Heaven Allows
Cunningham—Cocktails in the Kitchen
Depping—Blood, Sweat, and Tears
Dimmitt—Lili
Engle—Guys and Dolls
Esserman—Cocktails in the Kitchen
Estep—Shane
Gerlach—Picnic
Greve—National Velvet
Gutman—One Summer of Happiness
Guy—The Great Train Robbery
Haase—The Long, Long Trailer
Hardcastle—East of Eden
Harding—Mister Roberts
Hardy—Battle Cry
Harford—The Great Lover
Harrison—On the Waterfront
Haven—Lost Horizon
Hein—All That Heaven Allows
Herbst—Lady and the Tramp
Hockaday—Diabolique

Idol—Wild One
Jackes—The Man from Bitter Ridge
Jordan—Rebel Without a Cause
King—Snow White and the Seven Dwarves
Langenberg—Striporama
Levy—The Man with the Golden Arm
Magidson—Doctor in the House
McCarroll—Love Is a Many-Splendored Thing
McDonald—Picnic
McGinley—The Country Girl
McHaney—Diabolique
Metcalfe—Dragnet
Moran—Never Say Goodbye
Morrin—My Friend Flicka
Murphy—Mister Roberts
Pflager—All of Marilyn Monroe's
Rist, A.—Stalag 17
Rist, C.—Rear Window
Rogers—Harvey
Ross—The Ben Hogan Story
Ruwitch—Picnic
Schneeberger—The Man with the Golden Arm
Scholz—Harvey
Seddon—The Phantom from 20,000 Leagues Under the Sea
Stocker—East of Eden
Straub—Dolls and Guys
Terry—The Trouble with Harry
Thieme—Gone With the Wind
Wallas—Marty
Wattenberg—Mister Roberts
Weidemueller—One Summer of Happiness
Wulff—One Summer of Happiness

PROPHECY

Abel—taking over Davy "Nose Bold's" job
Baker—trying to get John Out of the bathtub
Beckers—still building crystal sets
Berger—telling the Hoff family not to ask silly questions
Bland—lady wrestler
Borders—cement-layer
Calkins—still trying to get caught up in physics
Clark—Queen of the Hoodesses
Conzelman—still procrastinating
Corrington—still playing the field
Cranston—Mrs. Christian Dior
Cullenbine—head coach at Burroughs
Cunningham—running the House with a large profit
Depping—stalled in her car
Dimmitt—another Sarah Bernhardt
Engle—Cool Cat's Combo
Esserman—still 6'2"
Estep—driving a Ferrari
Gerlach—manufacturing gloves
Greve—an English teacher
Gutman—happily driving a truck
Guy—buying his first car
Haase—still competing
Hardcastle—prima ballerina
Harding—making it rough for Bob Pettit
Hardy—still going to school
Harford—touring the Ozarks with a hillbilly show
Harrison—singing at the Met
Haven—leading a combined symphony and hillbilly show
Hein—still trying to get Clem to sell the jitney-bus
Herbst—fat-lady in a circus
Hockaday—drawing pictures of gizzards
Idol—head of the National Motorcycle Gang

Jackes—sitting around burning money
Jordan—still selling newspapers
King—in jail for using an alias
Langenberg—cashing in quiniela tickets
Levy—still single
Magidson—watching a cholangiocholecystocholedochectomy
McCarroll—not able to make up her mind who to marry
McDonald—taking three baths a day
McGinley—a squaw
McHaney—Mr. Laing's protégée
Metcalfe—with a new Ford
Moran—giving Jody money to burn
Morrin—a ripping butler
Murphy—playing pro-ball
Perkins—Twenty-five years from now, Tony finds himself as second understudy to Roddy McDowall.
Pflager—designing debut balls
Rist, A.—married to a policeman
Rist, C.—first woman pitcher for the Dodgers
Rogers—famous painteress
Ross—skinny-man in a circus
Ruwitch—still eating
Schneeberger—a state patrolman
Scholz—finally caught Mr. Eiseman
Seddon—sitting on top of Bevo Mill kicking the windmill around
Stocker—cleaning out the barn
Straub—singing with the Combo
Terry—sportscaster with KATZ
Thieme—C.P.A.
Wallas—bald
Wattenberg—making Havana cigars
Weidemueller—still hunting
Wulff—retired and driving in Florida

Advice to Seniors

NAME	SHOULD TRY TO
Erwin Bannenberg	Increase in height.
Addy Bayer	Keep up her genial temper.
Sarah Belowsky	Get over her timidity.
Mildred Bistorius	Keep up her kindly and charitable spirit.
Louise Born	Develop such hardy muscles as are required of a farmer's wife.
Cora Colby	Acquire the habit of boldness.
Gladys Erling	Make her influence felt everywhere.
Sarah Feder	Take the world not so seriously.
Alice Fowler	Make her cheerfulness felt by all.
Robert Franz	Appear livelier.
Agnes Gerstenberg	Show the real side of her nature.
Pearl Gilbert	Get a little more swing.
Helen Goppelt	Make herself a guiding light to all.
Mabel Hanson	Have her vivacity keep pace with her intellect.
Ralph Hantzsch	Continue to look down upon the world with a gracious smile.
Herman Huber	Develop his body as he did his mind.
Emil Jones	Wake up.
Pearl Katz	Adhere to the principle "Silence is golden."
Henrietta Kelling	Do her best to rival Maud Powell.
William Kickhaefer	Not to "kid" the public.
Laura Kleppe	Carry her quiet and lady-like methods thru the world.
Goldie Mabowehz	Not to let her philosophy get the best of her enjoyment in life.
Charlotte Marcus	Disclose her secrets of amiability to the world.
Frank Margoles	Not let his ambition usurp his pleasures in life.
Harry Margoles	Not allow people to impose too much upon his bigness of heart.
Harry Martens	Take the world as seriously as he takes football.
Sylvia Minner	Be happy and joyful.
Hertha Moritz	Continue her policy of honesty and sincerity.
Anita Oelke	Be more optimistic.
Eugenie Paulus	Should not let her actions be colored by her modesty.
Hasso Pestalozzi	Make his voice as manly as his thoughts.
Ruth Pipkorn	Widen her scope of friendship.
Florence Pollworth	Develop socially.
Norma Pusch	Continue her winning ways.
Elsie Reise	Make herself pleasant to strangers as well as to friends.
Rose Schefrin	Make her sweet voice a joy to the world.
Hyman Seidelman	Make his future life as successful as his high school life has been.
Joe Seidelman	Disclose his kindness of heart.
Eugene Shafrin	Follow his own mind.
Joe Sherr	Make the subject of modesty the study of his life.
John Steinhafel	Follow his artistic inclinations.
Hyman Sternlieb	Sow the seeds of joyfulness.

CLASS POLL

Class Actor, Class Pianist, Class Artist
Tony Perkins

Most Talented
Patricia Wilson and **Merald Knight**

Most Talented
Gladys Knight and Winston Meadows

Best-Looking
Susan Nixon and **Jimmy Hunter**

Who thinks he is the best student?
Goldstein.

Who think they are orators?
MacLeod and **Goldstein.**

Done school for most?
Hammond.

Gladys Knight

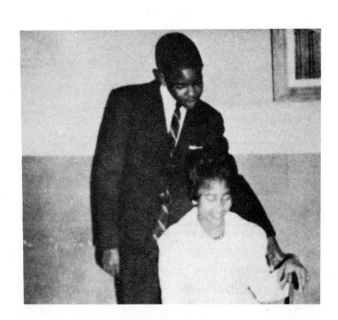

Merald Knight

Jimmy Hunter

Clem Henderson, **Faron Young**

Carrie Snodgrass, first.

135

BILL BLASS, 12B, HAS ALLERGY IN WHICH HE FACES HUNDREDS OF EGGS DURING EASTER TIME

Humpty Dumpty sat on a wall.
Humpty Dumpty had a great fall.
All the King's horses,
And all the King's men
Had scrambled eggs.

Not so with Bill Blass, 12B; by now he isn't able to tolerate an egg in any shape, form, or color. This egg allergy is seasonal with him. It comes on every year, about a week and a half before Easter, during which time he stares literally hundreds of eggs in their faces (and I do mean faces); that is, he has been so affected for the past six years previous to Easter Holidays. What we've been beatin' round the bush about is that Mrs. Blass' little boy, William, paints faces on hard-boiled eggs each Easter so parents will buy them for their little boys and girls who will consequently have reason to continue their belief in the Easter bunny (incidentally, Bill himself doesn't believe in him since entering upon the career of egg decorator).

The dates April 3 to April 9 didn't mean vacation to young Mr. Blass. They meant business and industry. His hours on the average were from nine to twelve, from one to six, and from seven to eleven. Occasionally, when it was necessary to speed up production, he followed an even tougher schedule. Acting as his own business manager didn't leave him any too much time for daydreaming either.

But now let's get down to the important topic, eggs. Here are some of the characters that our commercial artist has reproduced: the ever popular pair of mice—Mickey and Minnie—Donald Duck, the seven Dwarfs ('specially Dopey), crying babies, modern mademoiselles under cocky hats, Charlie McCarthy, Ferdinand the Bull, Matadors, Three Little Pigs, and oh, yes, Humpty Dumpty. He has found that he can always depend upon Walt Disney to create one of his lovable characters which he can reproduce on eggs with a great deal of business appeal. Last year it was Dopey, this year it was "the bull with a delicate ego."

Besides eggs and paint, nutcups, paper, lace, and other materials for hats, ties, ear, horns, and collars were used to prepare the hen fruit for their Easter parade.

Before painting, Bill used to sketch the face on first, but he became so good at applying the paint that he eliminated this process. He employs the use of another time-saver: mass production. He makes all those that are alike at the same time with brush strokes becoming mechanical. Mr. Blass finds it expedient, too, to paint oodles and oodles of noses, then oodles and oodles of eyes, and so on until a number of eggs are completed. He averages five minutes to an egg.

It was your reporter's pleasure to watch him in operation at a request demonstration. He seated himself before a potential Ferdinand and aptly created a nose. Then he stood up and shouted for a rag. This obtained, he gave the creature a pair of eyes. At this moment he decided he'd better put on his glasses, which he did. He continued to paint, giving Mr. Bull a mouth and some hair (yes, we learned Ferd has hair parted in the middle). It was at this point that he decided he didn't like to decorate eggs with people (yours truly was chaperoned by Mr. Bradbury) looking on. But at our very earnest request he resumed. Two ears were selected and adjusted to Mr. Bull's head; the two horns, and he was a full-fledged bull.

Then, too, there are the custom-made eggs. These are made up for special orders. For example, once for a dinner party for Mrs. Arthur Hall he painted the faces of her guests on eggs from pictures which she brought to him. He has an order pending to make purple and gold Mickey Mouses for a party to be given by Mrs. Carroll O'Rourke. Custom-made eggs are fifteen cents each, while the others cost ten cents.

Bill puts his eggs on display at information desks of a number of large offices, and someone there takes orders for him. An article published on the "Youths' Passing Show" page of the News-Sentinel about his egg industry caused a big boost in his sales.

The first year in business he realized a profit of $10, and the next $25. The last several years he made on the average of $50. This year he cleared $60 profit; sales of about 600 eggs.

At present Bill studies art under Miss Blanche Hutto at school. After his graduation he plans to attend art school in Chicago in an effort to prepare himself for work in commercial art.

The time for our interview was allotted because Mr. Blass was awaiting the arrival of twenty dozen eggs. At its close the telephone rang and he fell downstairs in anticipation of an order. It wasn't. But two members of The Times staff took the opportunity to depart and to escape further disillusionment (about the Easter Bunny).

JUNE 40'S WASHINGTON TRIP

The day had arrived. We had anticipated this date, Thursday, June 6, for months. This day we were to become pilgrims to Washington. We were to travel south, and the thought of this was thrilling, for the farthest south that most of us had ever been was the Navy Yard.

After boarding the streamlined train at the Broad Street station, the boys spent most of their time in planning exactly how to amuse themselves while in the Capital, and it would be quite incorrect to say that some of the suggestions were rather uninteresting.

We arrived in Baltimore at 10:25 A.M. and went directly to the buses which were to take us on a tour of Annapolis. Naturally, the "young gentlemen" went aboard the buses with dignity.

From the Naval Academy we went to Washington, stopping at the Franciscan Monastery, thence to the Supreme Court Building, which took out breath away, the Congressional Library, where our sacred Declaration of Independence is kept, and the United States Capitol, where an interesting tour of the building was made under the escort of special guides.

We left the Capitol at 4:30 P.M. in buses for the Lafayette Hotel. After a day like that the food at the hotel was absolutely delicious. Who will forget the amazement expressed on Mr. Gregory's countenance as he watched Dworkin and Berkowitz literally "eat the Lafayette out of business."

Friday, breakfast was at 7:45 A.M. The tune "How We Hate to Get Up in the Morning" did not apply to us that morning, for we were anxious to see everything possible.

Our first stop that morning was the Bureau of Engraving and Printing. It was here that we were struck by the only sad note of the trip. The irony of being so close to a hundred-thousand-dollar bill and yet not having it simply was too much for the boys.

The Washington Monument was the next item on our whirlwind tour. A few boys thought that it would be quite interesting to climb the stairs of this tall structure but they were soon discouraged. The majority took the convenient elevator. On no occasion had we ever seen a more beautiful panorama. Then in succession we visited the Pan-American Building, the Red Cross, and the White House.

The afternoon was spent in visiting the Federal Bureau of Investigation, Bureau of Fisheries, Arts and Industries Building, Aircraft Building, and the New Museum.

Valtri, Goodman, Giannuario, and Golden, as well as a number of others, seemed rather engrossed in the scenery other than that of historical interest.

On the spot, taking candid camera shots, was our good friend DiLello.

The diversions of the evening were just as interesting, if not more so, than those of the day.

Saturday, June 8, at 9:30 A.M., we went aboard sightseeing buses with our baggage for a tour of the city of Washington, stopping at the Zoological Garden, thence to Arlington National Cemetery, stopping at the Lee Curtis Mansion, and thence to Alexandria and Mt. Vernon, the picturesque home of the Father of Our Country. Here a few of the boys, Gatto, Rabiolo, and Gabler, tried the feat of throwing a dollar across the beautiful Potomac as Washington did. They finally agreed that George was a great man if he really had done it. However, the old saying must be remembered, and that is "A dollar went further in those days."

Returning to the Capital, the next stop was the magnificent Lincoln Memorial. If there is anything that will be remembered by the boys, it is the massive statue of Abraham Lincoln that is seen upon entering. We all agreed that this building was the most striking seen in Washington.

After visiting the National Academy of Sciences, we were taken to our last stop in Washington, the impressive and busy Union Station, where we entrained for home.

We shall never forget the beauty of the city of Washington, and shall always be proud of the memories of our National Capital.

Isn't It Grand?

Isn't it grand for us Seniors to forget school and its troubles,
To dream for a while of the days of yore when we were blowing bubbles?
When we washed our faces but forgot the soap in our eagerness to play—
For those were the days, the happy days when King Pleasure held his sway.

Isn't it grand to look back now and think of our foolish emotions?
How we feared the dark and the spooks at night, and hated those dreadful potions
Which fond mother gave us as she tucked us up, and kissed away our cares,
Then put out the light and left us alone and went down the creaking stairs.

Don't we remember our first day at school when mother dressed us in our best,
Then left us alone with the howling mob which put our courage to the test?
How we took our leave without a pass and cried our way to the street,
Where with a policeman's aid and guidance we beat a hasty retreat!

Can't we picture the day not long ago when we entered this Hall of Fame?
Can't we still feel the smart of the sharp retort and the sting of the words of shame
That were hurled at our defenceless heads for some task left undone,
For some new height left unscaled, for some laurel not won?

When we were Freshies weren't those Seniors grand and tall?
Their long pants and hats of felt were so admired by all.
And then it seemed so sudden, we had to take their place;
But once again we're Freshmen in this world that's ours to face.

Many a blow and many a knock will come to us through life;
And the quitter's the fellow who yields to them while struggling in the strife.
"Live and forgive"—is a motto that will make the path of fame
A bed of roses, whose fragrance will serve to ease the pain.

So we'll just take life as we find it, and smiling push our way through—
The friends we make will be many, the enemies scarce and few.
We'll keep the Southern spirit with a heart for anything,
And the walls of our dear Alma Mater forever our praises shall sing.

Just now we part; but golden years going by
Will find us all returning, Southern High.
Won't it be grand when, in the days to be,
We'll be swinging hand-in-hand down the lane of Memory?

HARRY POLIKOFF.

Illustration by
Jimmy Stewart

There's something dove-like about you.
You flatterer!!
Yes, you're pigeon-toed.

When you get
your diploma
signed & sealed, and bright
and new, may the success
be followed by many more:
And everyone add something
to make it a worthwhile i-cost.

Mother + Dad.

BUY
WAR BONDS
and
STAMPS

I take great pleasure in giving you a 65 this week. Oh, make it an 80 and enjoy yourself.

COMPLIMENTS

OF

A FRIEND

1940 POINSETTIA FINANCIAL STATEMENT

EXPENSES

Marcels for the Co-Editors	$ 55.45
Window shades (two pair)	4.21
Plug for key-hole	.05
Typewriter for circulation manager (slightly used)	2.00
Production costs for "Youth on Parade"	1245.92
Engravings	3.33
Printing	2.22
Covers	1.11
Wax for Mr. Bouchard's moustache	.97
Court fees for publicity manager	18.91
Loss from Senior Editors taking pictures	.80
New two-pants suit for ad solicitor Tallman	13.49
Medals for Business Manager (Lt. Entz to you)	145.00
Bribe to Mr. Byrleigh for Service Pins	350.00
To Board of Control for adopting budget	7.00
	$1234.56

INCOME

Received for flattering senior lines	927.00
Subscriptions from Student Body	47.80
Advertising (Thanks to the Bus. Staff)	3.72
Received from Carver for printing pictures	1200.00
Peeks at the dummy (Penny a Peek)	234.50
Income from "Youth On Parade"	.07
	$1234.56

Acknowledgements

I wish to thank Susan Hofmann for research; Joseph Berenis for preparing materials; Don Smith for his energy; and, especially, the hundreds of librarians, teachers and principals, friends and classmates, mothers and managers, who sought out and sent these all but forgotten yearbooks: Kenny Ambrose, Totty Ames, Marty Appel, Pat Argenio, Carl Auvil, Calvin Barnhart, Susan Beecher, David Belenzon, Gloria Bell, Lynn Bellehumeur, Norman Berger, Anthony DiBiasio, Jr., Robert Bodkin, Robert Boyce, Alice Brickner, Raymond Brocamp, Dee Brooks, Norma Brown, Michael Canepa, Donald Carmean, Penny Case, Diane Catalazzi, Max Cavalli, Robert Cheung, Gretchen Clarke, Billy Deaton, Judy-Lynn del Rey, Robert DiGiovanni, Hubert Dillworth, Dr. Hubert Eaton, Bill Esher, Lee Fishback, Anthony Foster, Mrs. Foster, Jane Gamble, Fred Garbrecht, Doc Giffin, Bob Goodman, Murray Goodman, Mrs. Greene, Clara Groehl, Phyllis Haigh, Mrs. Harris, Mrs. Hatcher, Herb Hellman, Esther Jacobs, Mrs. Johnson, Van Kaplan, Shirley Koenig, Aimee Kulp, Lorna Laspia, Eugene Light, Robin London, Brother Luke Lynch, Janet Meyer, Hughes Miller, Judy Montclare, Dan Moss, Natalie Pearlstein, Charles Pitro, Mark Pucci, Shirley Radder, Mrs. Robinson, Mrs. Rogers, Al Rosenberg, Charlie Rothschild, Ellen Rubin, Fern Salyer, Jack Silverman, Smitty, Mr. Spencer, Mrs. Tkach, Mrs. Truman, Pat Ugwudi, Ruth Wagner, Ann White, Mr. Wilkerson, Mary Wilson, John Yekikian.

Photo Credits: UPI, p. 18, p. 9.
Mercersberg Academy, p. 7, 63, 73, 78, 79, 85, 106, 132, 141, 142.

PUBLISHER'S NOTE

Photographic material created for publication in high school yearbooks is rarely preserved in its original form. Thus, most of the fabulous old photos in *The Yearbook Book* have had to be reproduced from scarce copies of the original yearbooks. It is for technical reasons related to the production processes involved that some of them exhibit an exaggerated half-tone dot effect.

Autographs

A light before my memory's shrine,
Your name upon this page shall shine.